David Philip Lindsley

The Elements of Tachygraphy

Third Edition

David Philip Lindsley

The Elements of Tachygraphy
Third Edition

ISBN/EAN: 9783337277246

Printed in Europe, USA, Canada, Australia, Japan

Cover: Foto ©Thomas Meinert / pixelio.de

More available books at **www.hansebooks.com**

THE
ELEMENTS OF TACHYGRAPHY.

ILLUSTRATING THE

FIRST PRINCIPLES OF THE ART,

WITH

THEIR ADAPTATION TO THE WANTS OF LITERARY, PROFESSIONAL, AND BUSINESS MEN.

DESIGNED AS

A TEXT-BOOK FOR CLASSES AND FOR PRIVATE INSTRUCTION.

BY
DAVID PHILIP LINDSLEY.

THIRD EDITION.

BOSTON:
OTIS CLAPP & SON, 3 BEACON STREET.
1873.

Entered, according to Act of Congress, in the year 1869, by
D. P. LINDSLEY,
In the Clerk's Office of the District Court of the District of Massachusetts.

Entered according to Act of Congress, in the year 1873, by D. P. LINDSLEY, in the Office of the Librarian of Congress, at Washington.

BOSTON:
Stereotyped by C. J. Peters & Son.

To

The Hon. Abijah Catlin,

OF CONNECTICUT,

WHOSE AID AND SYMPATHY PAVED THE WAY FOR THE FIRST

INTRODUCTION OF TACHYGRAPHY.

WHICH, WITHOUT HIS PATRONAGE, MIGHT HAVE BEEN

LONG BURIED IN OBSCURITY,

This Volume

IS GRATEFULLY INSCRIBED BY

THE AUTHOR.

PREFACE.

The system of *brief* writing, explained in the following pages, was mainly developed during the years 1857 to 1862. The delay in its publication has contributed somewhat to its perfection.

A brief and imperfectly-illustrated compend was published in 1864, which was so favorably received, even by men long trained in the old systems, and so generously commended by the most respectable portion of the public press, that the author was encouraged to labor for the fuller development of the system, and its general introduction, although such labor was a sacrifice he could not well afford to make.

Propagated, mainly, by the enthusiastic and unremunerated labors of those who have seen in the art, in its present simplified form, a new instrument for the elevation of the human race, it has spread, without attracting much public notice, aiding the student in preserving his lectures, the clergyman in preparing his discourses, as well as the verbatim reporter in his work.

Those who have cultivated it believe it capable of more extended usefulness. The author has been urged repeatedly, and by men from nearly all sections of the country, to provide a work sufficiently elaborate to furnish a complete guide to those who have no chance to secure the services of an instructor. Although he believes sincerely that a reliance upon books instead of teachers is false in theory, and likely to be unsatisfactory in its results, yet he has been compelled to acknowledge the propriety of providing teachers with better facilities than they have heretofore had.

This work is, then, prepared principally as a text-book, for use by competent and thoroughly-trained instructors; yet nothing has been omitted that was thought necessary to render it a complete guide to those who were compelled to rely entirely upon it.

In the first three chapters is given a brief illustration of those fundamental principles upon which the art must always rest. Some of these principles were understood many years ago by the better writers of the old systems; and those never fully incorporated in any previous system had been diligently sought for, and would be hailed with delight by writers who saw through the obscurity of their best efforts the brightness of a coming success, for which they could only pave the way. It is not proper that we should be filled with pride, who enter thus into the labors of others: it is more fitting that we should seek to exalt those who have borne the burden of cultivating a science that comes to fruitage only after several centuries have contributed to its growth.

The two great principles of continuity and lineality, secured in Tachygraphy by connective vowels and a skilful arrangement of the consonant letters, had been apprehended by some of the stenographic writers, but were overlooked by phonographers. But these principles could not be embodied in the old systems successfully. It was necessary that the accuracy first secured by Isaac Pitman, Esq., the noble inventor of Phonography, should be united to the severe simplicity of the best stenographies.

It was originally designed to give in notes the reasons

for deviating in all important cases from the practice of former writers, whether stenographers or phonographers. This has been done in a few instances; but it was feared that such details, that must be merely negative at best, would tend rather to embarrass than to aid the student.

The practice of the art commences with Chapter IV., in which is given the method of learning the alphabet, and of applying the new letters to the sounds they represent.

The writing exercises, commenced in Chapter VI., form a necessary part of the work. Only by writing these exercises, in connection with the study of the principles, can the student fully understand the text.

It has been thought better to introduce these writing exercises where they were needed by the student, than to add them as an appendix. In this we have consulted utility rather than the beauty of the work.

It was necessary, however, to place the reading-lessons in the end of the volume, because, being printed from engravings on copper, it was inconvenient to insert them in connection with the text they were designed to illustrate.

They were engraved by Mr. Chauncy B. Thorne, whose skill in engraving short-hand has done much to beautify the science in its older forms.

The wood-engravings scattered throughout the work are by the skilful hand of Mr. Richard B. Dyer of Boston.

It remains only to add, that this work is designed for ordinary practical men, who wish to gain the greatest speed in writing, with the least outlay of time and labor. Such men will, we trust, be satisfied with it. There are, however, two classes whose wants will not be fully met. The first are those who care little for speed, but desire to designate all the sounds in the language, and even in some foreign languages, with great accuracy. To accommodate these, a LIT-

ERARY STYLE was devised several years ago. But this class have not yet learned to rely upon short-hand to any great extent. If they ever demand such a style, it will be published. The second class will desire a briefer style, for verbatim reporting. For these, two briefer styles have been prepared (as yet unpublished), called the NOTE-TAKER'S, and the FAST REPORTING; the first capable of being written at the rate of a hundred and twenty to a hundred and fifty words a minute, and the second from a hundred and fifty to a hundred and eighty, or faster. But it must not be supposed that a person will necessarily write more rapidly in one of these styles than in the style given in the following pages. Men in the liberal professions, or in business, whose time is mainly engrossed in duties that render any especial attention to the mere *manner* of writing impossible, cannot retain a greater speed, ordinarily, than eighty to ninety words a minute; and this speed they will gain more surely in this style than in any other. If, dissatisfied with this, they cultivate a *reporting* style, instead of increasing their speed, as they hope to do, they will, in ninety-nine cases in every hundred, find themselves laboring through reporting contractions at the rate of forty to fifty words per minute, or even more slowly than this, and have the additional disadvantage of writing an *illegible* style. If such men really wish to increase their speed of writing, they can do it most certainly by adhering to the simplest forms, increasing their speed, as they do in the common writing, by great familiarity with first principles. They may in this way extend the power of the common style of Tachygraphy as here given, to almost any desired degree. Some students have found it adequate for nearly verbatim reports of lectures and sermons; and the author, after eighteen years' experience in the briefest contractions, finds this style best adapted to the work of a clergyman. The experience of many persons confirms this opinion. Among them the author is permitted to mention the Rev. A. T. Clark, who took an entire course of theological lectures, and now writes all his discourses, in the style taught in this volume, and has found it brief enough for all the purposes of note-taking. He prefers it to the briefer styles which he previously learned. The Rev. Peter Vogel gives similar testimony to the peculiar value of this style for the use of clergymen; and Mr. M. F. Tyler used it with the fullest success during his studies at Yale College and Law School, reporting, besides entire courses of lectures, sermons, conventions, &c. All these persons spent much time with briefer styles before falling back upon the plain and fully written forms; and such has been the experience of many others. Still there are some students, and some professional men, who will prefer the briefer forms of the NOTE-TAKER'S STYLE. Such persons are referred to the Second Part of this treatise, published, for convenience, in a separate volume.

Wishing the students of this little treatise a new life and joy in the truth and beauty of the principles here unfolded, it is commended to their love, with the ardent hope that it may give them leisure and ability to enter farther than they otherwise could have done into those beauties of science, opening on every hand, which speak of a Divine wisdom and love, inexhaustible and eternal.

THE AUTHOR.

CONTENTS.

	Page.	Sect.
INTRODUCTION	15	

CHAPTER I.

THE ORIGIN OF THE BRIEF LETTERS. 29

Straight Lines and Curves		5
Half-Circles and Dashes		9

CHAPTER II.

THE SOUNDS TO BE REPRESENTED. 33

Number of the Consonantal Sounds		13
Number of the Vowel-Sounds		14

CHAPTER III.

THE NEW LETTERS APPLIED. 34

Letters paired		23
Abrupts and Continuants		26
Lineality of Writing		27
Consonants grouped. — Labials, Lingua-Dentals, and Gutturals		28
Summary of Principles		29
Application of Principles		30
Signs for the Vocal Sounds		32

CONTENTS.

CHAPTER IV.

DIRECTIONS FOR PRACTICE. 44

Exercise on the Straight Signs	42
The Sounds of these Letters	44
Exercise on the Curved Signs	46
The Sounds they represent	48
The Liquids and *Ing*	51
Wa and *Ya*	52
Ja and *Cha*	53
The Direction in which the Letters are written	54
Size of the Letters	56
Variations of Vocal Signs	58
Size of the Vocal Signs	62

CHAPTER V.

METHOD OF JOINING THE LETTERS. 50

Connecting the Semicircles	65
Dash Letters	66
Diamond Points	70
The Joining of Full-sized Letters	72
Angles	73
Right Lines joined with Curves	74
The Joining of Curves. — Facing Curves	78–80
Opposing Curves	81, 82
Curves repeated	83
Straight Lines repeated	84
Vocals joined with Vocals	85
Disjoined Vocals	87
The Connecting Stroke	95

CHAPTER VI.

METHOD OF STUDY. 59

Writing Exercises	100
A Scheme for rendering the Sounds of the Old Letters more definite,	101

CONTENTS.

CHAPTER VII.

CONSONANTAL DIPHTHONGS. 69

Initial compounds, *L, R,* and *S* Series	106–7
Triphthongs	108
Qu and Compounds, with *W*	109
Wha and *Ha*	110
Final Compounds. — *L* and *R* Series	111
S Series	112
The Circle with the Small Dot Vowel	113

CHAPTER VIII. 80

The Omission of Vowels. Omission of Obscure Vowels in Long Words	114
The Omission of Vowels in Short Words of Frequent Occurrence .	115

CHAPTER IX.

PHRASE-WRITING. 85

Phrases determined by, 1st, The Convenience of the Writer; 2d, The Convenience of the Reader	116
Key to Paragraph 92, Reading-Lessons	116
Abbreviated Words and Phrases	117
Key to Paragraphs 93 and 94, pages 15 and 16 of Reading-Lessons .	117

CHAPTER X.

THE VARIABLE LETTERS. 90

Equivocal Word-Forms	118
Variable Letters	119
Em, El, Ar, Ma, La, and *Ra*	120
Special Cases	121
Ith and *The, Tha,* and *Qa*	122

CONTENTS.

Principles determining the Use of the Variable Letters . . . 123
   A. Right lines joined . . . .
   B. Right lines joined with Curves . . . .
   C. Curves joined with Curves. 1. Facing Curves. 2. Opposing Curves . . . .
Exercise Twenty-sixth . . . .
Key to pages 10 and 11, Reading-Lessons . . . . .

CHAPTER XI.
CONCLUDING INSTRUCTIONS.   96

Special Cases of Difficulty in Phonetic Spelling 124
Double Consonants . . . . 124 a.
The Letter *N* before *K*, *G*, &c. . . . . 124 b
The Letter *C* . . . . 124 c.
The Letter *X* . . . . 124 d.
Punctuation 125
Manual Drill 126
Exercise Twenty-seventh 126
Facility in Reading 127
Conclusion 128

APPENDIX.   103

The Position of Outlines 129
The New Sign for *Wha* 131
The Vowel *U*.—How Written 137
Abbreviated Forms for -*ness* and -*less* . . . . . 141 a.
The Use of the Circle with the Vowels ĕ and ŭ . . . . 141 b.
The Double Circle 142
The Prefixes *dis-* and *mis-* 143
The Termination -*son* . . . . 144 a.
The Termination -*ing* . . . . 144 b.

INTRODUCTION.

INVENTIONS are the levers that move the world. Every step in the advancement of mankind from barbarism to civilization is marked by the application of some new power, by which the force of body or of mind may be greatly augmented.

The puny arm of man has been relieved from nearly all kinds of drudgery by the power of water and of steam, and the ten thousand contrivances by which that power is applied. We have conquered matter, not by growing, as the fabled giants of old did, till we could pile mountain upon mountain by our unaided strength, but by learning how to apply, in a wonderful manner, the strength that God has given us.

Though we depend upon *facilities* to aid in mental and moral advancement, as much as in physical, yet we have been slow to apply to the mental and moral elevation of the race the principles that have enabled us to develop our material resources.

Inventions to aid in the commerce of ideas are no less essential than those which we have realized in the interchange of coarser commodities. The art of writing was the original lever by which the race was at first raised above barbarism. Successive improvements in this art have marked the epochs of the greatest mental activity.

The invention and use of short-hand writing paved the way for the introduction of Christianity, and aided its diffusion wonderfully. Verbatim reporters were common in the age of the apostles; and the sayings of the martyrs would never have been preserved without this instrumentality. Those heroic men who battled so nobly with pen as well as tongue in upholding Christianity against the wisdom of the Pagan world, relied, in some instances, on their staff of swift writers as a means without which they would have accomplished but little.

During the darkness of the middle ages, from the fifth to the fifteenth century, short-hand slept, and the intellect of the world slept with it; but, with the new life of the sixteenth century, short-hand revived, never, we trust, to be again obscured.

It would be necessary, to a full understanding of the present position of the art, to trace the gradual unfolding of its principles during the three centuries past. The devotion, zeal, faith, and patience that have been called out by the art are not surpassed in the records of any of the natural sciences. That the art is a science, with laws based in Nature, cannot be doubted by any one who studies its history, or even acquires its principles in accordance with its more rational forms of development. And, if any are discouraged by the long delay of its success, and the many failures that it has experienced, they should recollect that steam navigation and locomotion were as long unproductive of great results.

But we cannot here enter into the history of the art. It may be many years before the labor necessary to do justice to such a history can be employed to advantage. The pen seems to have been very chary of the records of its own achievements; and the great mass of men take the advantages of writing, even in the common form, as they do the air of heaven, without stopping to thank the Giver of all good, or to ask when, where, or how so wonderful a facility was discovered, who sacrificed their lives in its introduction, who aided its development, or how it gradually grew into its present form. In the glory of the results, we forget the instruments, and become insensible of our dependence upon them.

The advantages of brief and rapid writing may be made available in two ways; 1st, By the means of experts in its use, who act as reporters of popular assemblies, and amanuenses for literary men; and, 2d, By its general introduction among all classes of people.

The advantages of the art have been secured, to some extent, by reporters for the press, and by amanuenses; but this success is still partial. Less than one in ten of our newspaper reporters have heretofore been able to make the art available; while very few of our literary and business men seem conscious of the vast relief from toil, and the great augmentation of their power, that they might effect by the employment of short-hand writers. A business-man can, in this way, dictate answers to his correspondents in a few minutes, that would require five times as long to write out in the usual way; and thus save, at little expense, several hours of valuable time each day. And the literary man may dictate a work, not only with the freedom of extemporary discourse, but in a more satisfactory form than he could write it.

To the orator, whether discoursing on sacred or secular topics, this means of preparing discourses would, at least, treble his capacity for usefulness, and add to the freshness and vivacity of his discourses as much as to the ease of preparing them.

For these uses, the old and complicated forms of the art have answered to some extent. Though very imperfect for such uses, still, by a careful preparation of three to five years, young men of sufficient natural aptitude have become qualified for such service by the use of Phonography. Still, the introduction of the more facile and legible styles of Tachygraphy is demanded to render short-hand a complete success in *this* department of its use. The art cannot perform all that it is capable of doing, until all our newspaper reporters, and all our amanuenses and private secretaries, are able to bring it into their service. Most of them could not afford to spend the great amount of time and labor necessary to master the art in its previously-complicated forms; and besides, when they did devote years of labor to its acquisition, they found it too imperfect and illegible to answer perfectly the purpose for which they acquired it. But the labor of acquiring the art in its present form, as explained in the following work, is so greatly lessened, and its efficiency and accuracy so much increased, that all classes of amanuenses and newspaper reporters may avail themselves of its advantages.

But this is not the most important service which the art can render. Thought cannot live without expression. All acknowledge that education is, to a great degree, a drawing-out, or developing, of the faculties of the mind; and yet such are our educational facilities, that it is very difficult to do this. We are well supplied with books, and every facility necessary for furnishing mental food; but aids to mental *digestion* are few. Students in our schools are expected to put their own thoughts in order; but such is the labor and time required to perform the mechanical part of this work, that the active youth is soon disgusted with the effort.

But let all our students become skilful writers of Tachygraphy, and writing will be a pleasure, instead of a drudgery. The value of this means will, of course, depend largely upon the appreciation and skill of the teacher in using it; but, properly employed, it will add greatly to success in the higher departments of education. Especially in colleges and professional schools, lectures that are now forgotten as soon as heard will be preserved for use in afterlife.

This, however, is not the only use of the art in education. By converting what is now a drudgery into a pastime, a healthy mental activity is promoted. The passionate interest taken in the beauty and grace of the short-hand characters is such as is called out in the study of the *fine* arts, — painting, sculpture, and music.

There is still a broader field of usefulness for short-hand than the educational field. The art can never be useful to the highest degree, until all classes of people are instructed in its use. It will then be a social power wholly incalculable. We are strangers to the thoughts of our friends, and must remain so until this wonderful art shall unseal the fountains of affection, and bring those nigh that have been widely separated. Letters of friendship have grown few and brief. Correspondence has been mainly confined to business that must be done. All that is genial and invigorating in the interchange of thought has been frozen in the tediousness of utterance.

When Tachygraphy shall be generally known and used, an electric thrill of life will run through our communities, awakening new sympathies, and forming bonds of union long dissevered. What railroads have done in bringing friends together that could otherwise never interchange a visit during a lifetime, brief writing will do, in bringing *minds* together that would, without it, communicate with too much difficulty to be able to continue the acquaintance begun in youth; and aid in extending that more valuable interchange of thought among those of similar tastes, which tends both to the perfection of our knowledge of science, and its general diffusion.

Let us suppose, for illustration, that all mankind *spoke* with the slowness and painful effort with which we record language. Suppose we were obliged to spell every word by naming its letters, in order to talk; thus, I-n in, t-h-e the, b-e be, g-i-n gin, n-i-n-g ning, beginning, G-o-d, c-r-e-a-t-e-d, t-h-e, h-e-a-v-e-n-s, a-n-d, t-h-e, e-a-r-t-h, &c.: how long would conversation be tolerated in this age? Suppose, then, that this race of semi-mutes should be endowed with speech, with our present fluency; the new life that would burst forth in one universal shout of thanksgiving would indicate, in part, the rapture of the freedom introduced by the general use of brief writing.

The blessings of human speech are incomparably great. Nothing can take the place of that free and unfettered intercourse in which soul blends with soul. But speech dies on the air, and is lost; while writing may fly on the wings of the wind to any part of the earth, and may be preserved, if desired, for coming generations.

But, it may be asked, can this brilliant conception be realized? We answer, Most undoubtedly. It is not even a *difficult* thing any longer. The only difficulty was in the discovery of a really practical style of brief writing. This was difficult; for it required the growth of several centuries to bring it to perfection. But that difficulty has been finally removed. *Tachygraphy can be reduced to practice with far less labor than the chirography now employed.* If introduced to children at a proper age, they would become as proficient in its use, with one year's practice, as they now become in our common chirography with the labor of several years. Besides, it would be to them an inspiration and a joy, instead of a drudgery, and aid them to understand those general principles of language which are obscured by our present orthography.

The style best adapted to general use is fully written, and more legible than our present character. In its fullest form, it is written three times as rapidly as the common writing, while the *labor* saved is greater in proportion than the *time*. The hand is obliged, in Tachygraphy, to make only one-fifth as many strokes, and to move over only one-ninth the distance, in writing a given paper, that would be necessary in writing the same thing in the usual way.

The fully-written style of Tachygraphy, as illustrated in this volume, must not be confounded with those briefer styles designed for the use of reporters. We do not estimate here the speed and brevity of those more contracted styles; for they are not adapted for general use.

The use of stenographic contractions of any kind must always be limited; and the introduction of such styles, in connection with those of general utility, is to be regretted, as it gives occasion for the supposition that the art is mainly designed for such professional service.

In the styles of short-hand heretofore offered, legibility has been sacrificed to brevity, and the wants of the many to the demands of the professional reporter. But these works have professed to offer advantages to all, and have been eagerly sought for by all classes of people. Though we have no means of making accurate statistics on this subject, yet, from the enormous sale of some editions of the text-books on Mr. Pitman's phonography, we have reason to believe that at least half a million of text-books have been sold during the past twenty-eight years.* Half a million of experiments would satisfy any scientist as a basis for generalization. Now, what does the result show in favor of the attempt to introduce stenographic peculiarities for the general purposes of writing? Probably not more than five hundred persons of the five hundred thousand persons procuring these works have become really expert in the use of them. One in every thousand has attained the skill sought for in the use of a style adapted only to reporters.† Perhaps five hundred, or possibly a thousand more, have gained a degree of speed equal to what they might have acquired in a simpler, plainer style; while at least four hundred and ninety-eight thousand failed to make it answer the end for which they sought it. Must the millions be deprived of this art simply because they cannot thread the mazes of the arbitrary contractions designed for professional reporters? Such a conclusion would be no more reasonable than to assume that it was impossible to found a city, because it was found impossible to draw together a very large number of persons on the top of the White Mountains; or to deny that a railroad was practicable after a mountain had been tunnelled, simply because no train of cars could be drawn over its highest peak.

The author of Tachygraphy has continually endeavored to keep within the bounds of actual achievement in stating the capacities of the art. Those who have spent much time in the study of Phonography, to but little purpose, may still make this study productive, by applying the knowledge of

---

* Most of these works were published in England. Probably, however, two hundred and fifty thousand copies have been sold in this country, counting those published here and imported from England.

† Though the author has not been able to collect entirely accurate details on this subject, yet he has gathered facts from teachers of Phonography, that give a degree of definiteness to these estimates. The facts are too notorious to be doubted by those who have attended to the subject.

the principles of the art gained in this way to the practice of Tachygraphy. Those who have spent from five to twelve years in the practice of Phonography have found, that, so far from being hindered by this in acquiring Tachygraphy, their previous practice of a different style was a great aid to them. When the hundreds of thousands who have invested in Phonography a capital of labor that is not now available shall follow the example of those who have already tested the matter, they will find that their former painful labor has become highly productive; and that the years which they had counted lost are restored again with an unexpected increase.

Experience is more reliable than theory; and the practical success of a particular method is of more value than any explanation of the philosophy by which that success is gained. Yet the seductiveness of brief forms, attained at no matter how much sacrifice of simplicity or legibility, is so great, that those with but little experience are very likely to be deceived. There is something fascinating in the beautiful devices for contraction, that leads the student forward step by step; and he is unwilling to leave any thing unlearned that the science renders possible. So far as this is a mere matter of taste, so far as it is a passion for science, it is to be praised; but, if the student memorizes a greater number of details than he can command readily, they burden the mind, hinder speed in writing, and finally lead to disgust and failure. Modes of contraction that seem very easy to the enthusiastic student, when his mind is engrossed by the science, become far more difficult to employ when the distracting cares of business or other studies occupy the attention. But he is not likely to understand this at the time; and when, in later years, experience teaches him his error, it is too late for him to rectify his mistake: he must abandon a style too cumbersome to be endured, and has, too frequently, no leisure to master a simpler. If those who have made the experiment with Phonography will testify to their experience, as large numbers have already done, they will save many young persons from such a waste of time and effort; but we ask no testimony of those who have used the art but a short time, and are still bewildered by its deceptive promises.

We have felt it a duty to offer this word of caution, not merely to guard the inexperienced against the old forms of the art, but also to warn the student against attempting the reporting style of Tachygraphy, without first counting the cost, and considering carefully the probability of its being as well adapted to his purpose as the simplest style. While the reporting style of Tachygraphy is much more easily acquired, and much more legible, than Phonography, yet it should not be attempted by those who are not prepared to make its use their principal business, at least for a term of years.

Students in academies and colleges who contemplate an extended course of education may master the note-taker's style to advantage, for the purpose of taking more accurate notes of the lectures of their proposed courses of study. But, when fairly engaged in their professions, they will be quite likely to drop all contractions, and write the art in its simplest form.

There is one other caution, that we would make so emphatic, if possible, that no student of the art should ever forget it. It is this: On no account attempt to write *two styles* of the art. Any one that should attempt to preserve his knowledge of Phonography while cultivating Tachygraphy would most certainly fail. Let the decision made in favor of the style used be *decisive*.

The same caution applies to the effort to write a more or less contracted style of the same system. It cannot be done, except at a great sacrifice of facility in both styles. Teachers are sometimes compelled to do this to accommodate their writing to pupils of different degrees of proficiency; but they must be content with a comparatively low rate of speed.

These suggestions are offered to those who wish to make the art *useful.* If any cultivate it for amusement, and speculate in different styles from a love of variety, we trust they will accept the result of their choice, without making us responsible for their success in acquiring skill in rapid writing. We would not discourage an appeal, on the part of the teachers of Tachygraphy, to that love of the beautiful, which must always be an attractive charm, winning more to the culture of the art than even its great and acknowledged utility can do. This love ought to be encouraged as an ennobling influence, leading the mind to an appreciation of all true art, and through this to divine excellence. But let that appeal be made to the greater beauty mingling with the severe simplicity of the fuller forms of the art, rather than to those accidental devices which break the true harmony of the science. Educate the taste until irregular forms shall be offensive.

FOREIGN LANGUAGES.

The alphabet of Tachygraphy was arranged with especial reference to its application to foreign languages. Some adaptation will be necessary to make it as useful in German, French, and other European languages, as in our own; but this was originally designed, and provision was made for such additions as would be necessary, so that the harmony of the system might remain when it should be adopted by other nations.

The best systems of short-hand have heretofore appeared in the English language. Nearly all the true principles of the science would seem to be of English discovery and development. And yet, with all their rudeness, the German systems seem to have been more generally employed, on account of their greater simplicity. It is hoped that the introduction of Tachygraphy will show that those who use the English language are not only able to discover the true principles of the science, but to apply them successfully to practical use.

Let it be known that there is but one *science* of brief writing for all nations, as there is but one science of mathematics, one true philosophy of human liberty, one true religion, and one God, and the general introduction of that system which best embodies the *science*, will pave the way for that universal language which must yet bind into closer relations the whole family of man.

PRELIMINARY DIRECTIONS.

WRITING-MATERIALS.

A steel pen is the best instrument for writing short-hand. Some gold pens will answer; but they are not apt to be stiff enough for this use.

As a reporter is sometimes compelled to use a pencil, some practice in this way is necessary; but, when a pencil is used, it is necessary to have unsized paper.

MANNER OF HOLDING THE PEN.

In the common writing, the principal strokes are backward, while in Tachygraphy they are mostly inclined forward. This renders a change in the manner of holding the pen desirable.

The pen, when writing Tachygraphy, should be held between the first and second fingers. It should be steadied by the thumb as it is when held in the usual way.

Tachygraphy may be written on either ruled or unruled paper by the experienced writer; but the learner will find it convenient to have ruled paper in his earlier exercises, for the same reason that ruled paper is convenient in learning to write in the common way.

EXPLANATION OF TERMS.

VOCALS. — The short-hand letters which represent the sounds of vowels are called *vocals*, or *vocal signs*.

CONSONANTALS. — Those representing consonant sounds are called *consonantals*.

OUTLINE; WORD-FORM. — The form a word assumes when written with the short-hand characters.

TACHYGRAPHY (pronounced *ta-kig'ra-fy*). — Greek ταχυς (*tachus*), rapid; and γραφή (*graphe*), writing, — rapid writing.

PHONOGRAPHY (*fo-nog'ra-fy*). — Greek φωνή (*phone*), sound, or voice; and γραφή, writing, — the writing of the sounds of the human voice. The word *phonography* is generally used to designate the system of short-hand writing invented by Mr. Isaac Pitman, of England. It is, however, sometimes used in a more extended sense, for any kind of character that assumes to express the elements of spoken language.

CALLIGRAPHY (*ka-lig'ra-fy*). — Greek καλλιγραφία (*kalligraphia*), fine or beautiful writing.

PHONETIC or PHONIC. — Greek φωνή (*phone*), voice, — pertaining to the expression of the sounds of the voice in language. A phonetic system of writing is one which expresses the sounds of the language. All the languages of Europe, and most of the languages of Asia, as well as the English language, of the present, and the Latin, Greek, Hebrew, and Sanscrit, of the past, are written phonetically. The ancient languages are written with great phonetic precision; but some modern languages have departed, to a greater or less extent, from this basis.

PHONETICS. — The science which treats of the phonic representation of language.

ELEMENTS OF TACHYGRAPHY.

CHAPTER I.

THE ORIGIN OF THE BRIEF LETTERS.

1. In reconstructing our written characters, the first problem to be solved is, On what principle shall we select briefer and better letters?

It would not do to attempt to abbreviate our present writing by omitting a part of each letter; for this would result in confusion and illegibility.

2. If, for instance, we should attempt to shorten the letter *m* by omitting the last angle, we should make the letter *n;* and if we abbreviate *n* in the same manner, we make *ι*, a mere undotted *i*.

This process would not do with any of the letters; and yet it is impossible that we should continue to make, as we do now, four or more strokes of the pen for each letter, if one stroke can be made to answer the same purpose.

3. But there is another method of abbreviating the old letters, viz., by omitting the strokes that unite them together. Thus, instead of *a*, *b*, *c*, *d*, &c., we could write *a, b, c, d,* &c. But we should not gain in ease of

writing by this; for this is the way the ancients wrote: and we have found that we can write faster by joining the letters together, even if we use more strokes in writing. So we will not attempt to go back to a style that was abandoned several hundred years ago.

4. We shall have to lay the old letters aside; but what kind of letters shall we employ in their place? It takes time and labor to make marks with a pen: so we must get brief and easy signs. Besides, letters must be joined to one another in many ways. They must be, then, *regular* lines, so that a boy or girl that has studied geometry can tell just the angle that any two letters would make when joined. In this way, we shall have a *science*, a *mathematical science*.

We will take the simplest regular characters. 1. *Straight lines.* 2. *Curved lines.* 3. *Brief dashes.* 4. *Dots.*

STRAIGHT LINES AND CURVES.

5. We must be careful to keep a sufficient difference between the letters. Suppose we take four light lines like these \ | /, and four heavy ones in the same direction \ | /. This gives us eight very simple letters.

6. We will now make curved lines, of the *quarter* of a circle, in the same directions as the straight lines above. We can curve them either way. In the direction of —, we have ⌒ and ⌣; in the direction of \, ⌐ and ⌙; in the direction of |,) and (; in the direction of /, ⌒ and ⌒.

7. In this way we get eight more letters formed with light characters; and can make eight more by

HALF-CIRCLES, DASHES, AND DOTS.   31

making heavy letters corresponding to them, thus ; ⌒ ⌣) (⌒ and ⌣.

We may get these signs from dividing a circle, as seen in the illustrations on the fifth page of the reading exercises in the end of the book.

8. In this way we get twenty-four letters, each made of a single straight or curved line. They have a positive, fixed direction, and regular form: so that we can always know just what the angle will be when they are joined together, or whether they join without making an angle.

HALF-CIRCLES, DASHES, AND DOTS.

9. The old stenographers made large *half-circles*, instead of quarter-circles, for their large letters. This was inconvenient. But semicircles, when very small, are convenient and distinctive. We will make them only about one-fifth the size of the lines and curves selected in paragraphs 5-7.

By dividing a circle horizontally and perpendicularly, we get ⌒ ⌣ ⊂ ⊃ heavy, and ⌒ ⌣ ⊂ ⊃ light, — eight. Now let us take short strokes, only one-fifth as long as before given, and in the same directions, and we get - \ ׀ ⁄ heavy, and - \ ׀ ⁄ light, — eight more.

10. There remain, of the simple characters chosen, only the dots. They are less useful than any of the others, because they cannot be joined in writing. We are more plagued in our old writing by the necessity of dotting the *i* and *j*, and crossing the *t*, than by the almost interminable *m*. But we will venture to take two dots, a heavy dot and a light one [. and .].

NOTE. — The use of the signs given above, in place of the old letters, is not only theoretically plausible, but has proved to be practically successful. They have formed the foundation of most of the systems of short-hand that have appeared during the past century in England and America. There is no question now, among intelligent students of the art, as to the elementary signs that must form the basis of a practicable system of brief writing. All respectable modern writers on the subject accept the use of quarter-circles, and right lines (distinguished by direction), and dashes, dots, and semicircles, as the only proper and feasible letters to be used in brief writing.

There remains, however, a difference of opinion between modern writers concerning the particular sound or sounds which each new letter, or group of letters, should represent. So far, then, we have followed principles developed by previous writers, — principles that have been eliminated slowly by the experience of centuries.

But there are still works on short-hand extant, in which these principles do not appear. The system most used in Germany would seem to be based on an alphabet totally devoid of method or design, a relic of the rudest stage of the art; and some English and American authors have deviated, in the selection of their alphabetic characters, so far from natural principles, as to give their readers an impression that short-hand was a mere collection of arbitrary symbols.

We trust, however, that the art has at last a scientific basis; and that, whatever changes may occur in details, its foundation-stones will never again be removed.

CHAPTER II.

THE SOUNDS TO BE REPRESENTED.

11. LETTERS represent the *elements* of speech, and there should be a letter to represent each elementary sound in the language. This is not the case with our present orthography. We have only twenty-six *letters* to represent *thirty-six* elements.*

Three letters, *c*, *q*, and *x*, represent sounds for which we have other representatives: *c* sounds like *k*, *s*, or *sh ;* *q* like *k ;* and *x* like *ks* or *gz*. This leaves only *twenty-three* letters for thirty-six sounds.

12. The thirteen sounds for which we have no letters, in the old orthography are expressed, —

1st, By giving each of the vowels, *a*, *e*, *i*, *o*, and *u*, more than one sound each ; as, for instance, *a* in *ale*, *all*, *at* and *arm ; o* in *ore*, *on*, and *done*, &c.

2d, By making digraphs, such as *th*, *sh*, *ch*, *ng*, which express, when combined, sounds entirely different from what they express singly.

3d, By appropriating a letter that generally expresses one definite sound to another sound, either allied to it or wholly dissimilar ; as in the case of *s*, which is used for *z* and for a sound heard in *azure*, that has no proper letter of its own.

* We can easily make more than thirty-six sounds by counting every variety; but we only wish here to illustrate the general principles of pure phonics, without entering into details. Orthoepists differ widely in their estimate of the number of sounds in our language; but those that count the least make the number thirty-six.

NUMBER OF THE CONSONANTAL-SOUNDS.

13. We cannot pause here to enter into the matter fully; but a little examination will show that we have twenty-four consonantal sounds, represented in our ordinary writing by *b, d, f, g, h, j, k, l, m, n, p, r, s, t, v, w, y, z, ch, sh, th* (in thy), *th* (in thin), *ng,* and one that has no letter, and no combination of letters appropriate peculiarly to it; viz., that written with a *z* in *azure,* and with an *s* in *pleasure.*

NUMBER OF THE VOWEL-SOUNDS.

14. Here we may find more difficulty; for some vowel-sounds are not clearly distinguished in our ordinary conversation, so that they become obscure. So, to simplify the matter, we will omit all obscure sounds, and take only those that every one can distinguish without difficulty.

15. We have *a, e, o,* long, and *a, e, i, o, u,* short; *a* as in *far,* and another *a* in *fall; oo* in *moon; u* in *full; o* in *or; ai* in *air;* and the diphthongal sounds *i* and *u* long, *oi* and *ow,* — eighteen in all.

CHAPTER III.

THE NEW LETTERS APPLIED.

16. We have found (6, 7, 8) twenty-four straight lines, and curves of the quarter of a circle, and (13) twenty-four consonantal sounds. We have also (9, 10)

eighteen small half-circles, dashes, and dots, and eighteen vocal sounds.

17. It is quite appropriate to honor the consonantal sounds with full-sized characters, because the consonants are the principal elements in words. Vowels give the different shades of meaning which the same root-word assumes; but the consonant forms the enduring and important part of the word.

18. Besides this, it would be very awkward to mix up these signs, representing some consonants by full-length characters, and others by small signs; for the difference between a vowel-sound and a consonant-sound is very great, and should be distinctly marked in an accurate system of writing.

19. We have, then, just enough large signs to represent the consonant-sounds, and just enough small signs to represent the vocal sounds. We have a very good reason, besides the fact that the numbers correspond, for preferring the large signs for the principal elements in the word, and the small signs for the vocal elements (17, 18).

20. So far, we find very beautiful results and easy progress. The simplest strokes possible — *lines, curves, dashes,* and *dots* — can be so arranged as to furnish all the signs we need. They are so brief and beautiful, that it is a wonder that our wise ancestors ever thought of using any others in their writing. But to what individual sound shall we wed each individual sign? Shall we make a perpendicular or inclined or horizontal sign for *b?* Shall it be light, or heavy? Shall it be curved, or straight? We have only determined to take the twenty-

four full-sized characters first introduced for the consonantal signs, and the eighteen small letters for the vocal signs; but we see no reason yet for preferring one of these signs to another for any given sound.

21. REMARK. — If we can find no principle to guide us here, we may experiment in vain. If we should ring all the changes possible by the laws of permutation on only twenty-four characters, we might make more than six hundred and twenty sextillions of alphabets, each differing by one letter from the other; while if a wider selection of letters is made, with no more regard for principle than some writers have had, the permutation, based on forty or fifty signs, instead of twenty-four, would yield a number of possible alphabets many billions of billions of times greater than the number above stated.

22. And, if any one is anxious to press these possibilities further, he should consider that each alphabet may form the basis of many conflicting systems, as is shown in the so-called phonography, and the previous systems of stenography; so that an alphabet built solely on *experiment* is impossible: for all mankind might make alphabets, during all the ages of the world, and each make a thousand alphabets, without exhausting the *possibilities* of improvement. The famous Labyrinth of ancient Crete, with its "thousand halls and thousand winding ways," was not at all comparable to such an endless confusion as would result from the effort to establish an alphabet on a purely *empirical* basis.

Let us, then, see what principles, if any, we can find to guide us through this labyrinth of labyrinths.

LETTERS PAIRED.

23. We find, first, that most of the consonant-sounds may be arranged into *pairs* of two letters, which are formed by the same organs, and differ only in being more or less *vocal*. Thus, *b* and *p* are formed by the lips in the same position; but *b* is more vocal than *p*. So

d and *t*, *g* and *k*, *v* and *f*, &c., may be paired in a similar manner.

Now, we find it natural to represent each of these vocal sounds *b*, *d*, *g*, *v*, &c., by heavy signs; and each of the whispered or aspirate sounds by light signs.

24. This principle has many considerations in its favor. If similar sounds are represented by similar signs, there is less danger of mistake in reading; for if a *p* is read for a *b*, or a *t* for a *d*, the sense would be clear. Mr. Isaac Pitman, author of Phonography, has illustrated this principle by the following sentence: *Buy wisdom and get knowledge, and prize them as the greatest treasure.* The short-hand letters for *b*, *d*, *g*, *s* (in prize), *th*, &c., would be heavy; but if a careless writer should make them all light, making a mistake in every word, the sentence would read, *Puy wistom ant ket knowletch, and price them as* (s) *the createst treashure*, which sounds a little Teutonic, but is perfectly intelligible.

So this method of pairing the characters and the sounds of the letters enables us to use signs differing only in the thickness or shading of the stroke, without danger of illegibility.

25. It will be seen that we have given the shaded or heavy sign to the most audible sound. This is because a light stroke is more easily made than a heavy one; and the whispered sounds are of more frequent occurrence than the rougher sounds: so that, by making this arrangement, we represent the most frequently-occurring sounds by the letters which are made the most easily.

NOTE. — Some persons, ignorant of the practice of the art, have thought that the use of shaded letters might be avoided.

But, before this subject can be considered, we must discover twelve other letters, *simpler* and more feasible. The experience of many thousands of persons, of all grades of talent and skill, has demonstrated the practicability of this arrangement. All the systems of Phonography are built on this basis.

26. In this way, *order* begins to emerge from the *chaos* that confronted us.

It will be seen, by considering the nature of the sounds further, that six of them, *b, p, g, k, d,* and *t*, are spoken abruptly; while the sounds of others, such as *v, f, z, s,* &c., may be drawn out, or continued at pleasure. So it seems quite natural to give the straight signs to these abrupt sounds, and the curves to those more flowing.

There are other reasons for this arrangement that cannot be explained without a further knowledge of the principles of the art, and we must leave them to be discussed elsewhere.

LINEALITY OF WRITING.

27. But we observe, further, that some of our new letters | |)) ((\ \ ⌊ ⌊ ⌉ ⌉ can be best struck downward; and facility in writing demands that they should be joined together in writing. If, then, it should happen that the sounds occurring most frequently were represented by letters running downward, we should get very unmanageable word-forms. Suppose, for instance, we should make | stand for *d*, and other letters as follows, | *t*, \ *b*, \ *p*, / *j*,) *z*,) *s*, &c., and should then try to join these letters into such a word as "disad-

SUMMARY OF PRINCIPLES.

vantageous." Omitting the vowels, we should have This would never do. It would run down so far as to hinder the writing of the next line. Besides, if it were found that certain sounds recurred in the language much more frequently than other sounds, we could avoid this difficulty by giving the horizontal signs to the most frequently-recurring sounds; for the horizontals might run on across the page without causing any difficulty. Now, it is found that the sounds of *d*, *t*, *z*, *s*, and *n*, occur more frequently than any others. By giving these sounds the horizontal signs — — ⌒ ⌒ and ⌣, we can write *disadvantageous* thus

28. We have one more grand principle. Certain sounds are made chiefly with the lips, and are called *labials;* others are made chiefly with the palate, and are called *palatals;* and others with the tongue and teeth, and are called *lingua-dentals*.

The law of analogy leads us to class sounds made by the same organs together: so we write the labials by perpendicular signs, palatals by slanting signs, and lingua-dentals by horizontal signs.

SUMMARY OF PRINCIPLES.

29. We have, then, three great laws upon which to arrange the full-length strokes:—

(*a.*) *Analogy between the sounds and signs*, leading us to give to sounds differing only in a greater or less vocality signs differing only in shading, and to give sounds made with the same organs signs in the same direction.

(*b.*) *A law of harmony*, by which abrupt sounds have signs equally unbending, and more flowing sounds more flexible signs.

(*c.*) *A regard to lineality.* We gain lineality and facility of writing by giving those groups of sounds that occur most frequently horizontal signs. This last feature alone is peculiar to this system. The principles mentioned in *a* and *b* are found also in the various systems of Phonography.

APPLICATION OF PRINCIPLES.

30. Applying the above principles, we find most of the new letters fall very naturally into their places as follows:—

$$| \quad | \quad \diagdown \quad \diagdown \quad - \quad - \quad) \quad) \quad \frown \quad \frown \quad \smile$$
$$b \quad p \quad g \quad k \quad d \quad t \quad v \quad f \quad z \quad s \quad n, \text{ &c.}$$

ANOMALIES.

31. But still some perplexing questions occur; for no science falls so completely into order and harmony as to render human ingenuity useless. We have three letters, *h, w,* and *y,* that seem to be scarcely consonants at all, and deserve separate treatment. We have four letters, *m, n, l,* and *r,* that cannot be paired, as *b* and *p* are, with any other sounds in the language; then we have the nondescript sound *ng,* and the semi-compound *ch,* and *j,* all of which anomalies demand attention. But these little difficulties are easily reduced to some assignable limits.

We have a frame-work, and must leave the student to fill up the outline for himself, or consult the alphabet for further particulars.

SIGNS FOR THE VOCAL SOUNDS.

32. We have assigned the small signs given in paragraphs 9, 10 to the vocal sounds. It remains that we assign particular classes of these signs to particular classes of sounds.

We shall be obliged to treat of this matter briefly, and shall mention such distinctions only as are made use of in forming the alphabet.

Vocal sounds are either,
(1) Long or Short;
(2) Labial or Palatal;
(3) Simple or Diphthongal.

33. Long sounds are represented by heavy or shaded signs; and the short sounds corresponding to them by the analogous light signs. And here it should be observed that the short sound most resembling *e* long is not *e* short, but *i* short; and the sound of *a* long shortened approximates more nearly to that of *e* short in *ebb* than to that of *a* short in *abb*.

34. The sounds represented by the light vocal signs must not be considered as differing only in quantity from those represented by the corresponding heavy signs; for there is also a slight difference in quality.

PALATAL VOWELS.

35. Vocal sounds, as well as consonantal, may be classed with reference to the organs principally used in

uttering them. Those formed in the back part of the mouth, called *palatals*, or *gutturals*, are the long sounds heard in *eve, ale, are,* and *air;* and the corresponding short sounds heard in *it, ebb, add.* These we have represented by the semicircular and dot signs ⌒ c . ᴜ ᴖ . ᴜ

36. Those vocal sounds formed near the front part of the mouth by the use of the lips, called *labials*, are heard in the words *ooze, ore, all, foot, up, on.* They are represented by the dash signs - ı ⁄ , - ⟍ ⁄ .

DIPHTHONGS.

37. The long sounds of *i* and *u* are considered diphthongal, and are represented by the diamond points ᴠ and ᴧ respectively.

The open diphthongs *oi* and *ow* are written by the union of the signs of their component parts. Thus, *oi* is composed of ⁄ and ⌒, and is written ɼ or ᴠ ; and *ow* is composed of ⁄ and -, and is written ⁄ or ᴧ ; the direction of the second stroke being changed to make a more acute angle.

We add, on the following page, a complete alphabet of all the new letters, with the sounds they represent.

THE ALPHABET OF TACHYGRAPHY.

CONSONANTAL SIGNS.

SIGN.	NAME.	SOUND.	SIGN.	NAME.	SOUND.
|	Be,	b in bay.	⌐	The,	th in they.
|	Pe,	p in pay.	⌐	Ith,	th in oath.
\	Ga,	g in go.	⌒	Em,	m in may.
\	Ka,	k in key.	⌣	En,	n in nay.
—	De,	d in do.	⌣	Ing,	ng in sing.
—	Te,	t in to.	)	El,	l in lay.
)	Ve,	v in eve.	/	Ra,	r in ray.
)	Ef,	f in if.	⌒	Wa,	w in we.
(	Zhe,	z in azure.	⌒	Ya,	y in ye.
(	Ish,	sh in show.	⌒	Ha,	h in high.
⌒	Ze,	z in ooze.	⌐	Ja,	j in jail.
⌒	Es,	s in so.	⌐	Cha,	ch in each.

VOCAL SIGNS.

⌒	E, e in eve.		⌒	ĭ, i in it; y in duty.
c	A, a in ace.		·	ĕ, e in ebb.
·	Ai, ai in air.		⌣	ă, a in ask, at.
⌣	Ah, a in are.		–	ŏŏ, oo in foot; u in full.
–	Oo, o in do.		\	ŭ, ŭ in us, fun, but.
|	O, o in ode.		/	ŏ, o in on, or
,	Au, au in aught.		v	I, i in ice.
⸝	Oi, oy in boy.		ʌ	Ew, ew in dew.
,	Ow, ow in now.			

CHAPTER IV.

DIRECTIONS FOR PRACTICE.

38. Having, then, an alphabet of the simplest characters, the next step is to learn to use them with freedom and grace, as we do the old letters. It is first necessary to commit them to memory, so as to form them with ease, and read them at sight.

39. This can be done best by writing the letters in pairs, commencing with | | | | | | | | , &c., repeating them twenty to thirty times. Take care to make them exactly perpendicular and of the proper length, — one-sixth of an inch. Make them of an even thickness throughout, of equal length, and parallel to each other.

40. It will be well to speak the sound as you make the letter that represents it. This will enable you to associate the letter with its proper sound.

41. Do not attempt to learn the whole alphabet at once, but master two letters at a time.

After learning | |, add \\, observing their direction as before. Then proceed in a similar manner with — —, as follows :

EXERCISE ON THE STRAIGHT SIGNS.

42. *b, p* | | | | | | | | | | |, &c., repeated throughout the line.

g, k \\\\\\ \\\\\\ &c., repeated throughout the line.

EXERCISES. 45

$d, t ===$, &c., repeated throughout the line, or
— — — — — — — | | | | \\ | | \\ — —, &c.

NOTE. — 43. It will be well to trace the characters throughout the work with an ivory point; but this method of practice should never detract from the use of the pen, because the student needs to train his eye to accuracy, and develop his taste and judgment, which cannot be done by mere imitation of printed forms.

THE SOUNDS OF THESE LETTERS.

44. | | — and — have the sounds always represented by *b, p, d,* and *t.* \\ has the sound of *g* heard in *go, beg,* but never the sound of *j,* or *g* soft, heard in *gem.* \\ has the sound of *k,* and the identical sound of *c* hard in *come.*

NOTE. — *G* soft is represented by ⌣ ; and *c* soft, by ⌢.

45. After thoroughly mastering these letters, proceed in a similar manner with the curves, observing that the heavy curves are shaded only in the middle, and taper towards each end.

EXERCISE ON THE CURVED SIGNS.

46. *v, f*))))))))))))
    zh, sh ((((((((((((((
    z, s ⌢ ⌢ ⌢ ⌢ ⌢ ⌢ ⌢ ⌢
    th, th ╲ ╲ ╲ ╲ ╲ ╲ ╲ ╲

THE SOUNDS THEY REPRESENT.

47.)) ⌢ and ⌢ represent the sounds of the letters *v, f, z,* and *s,* as given in the alphabet. It need only be

observed that the letter *s* in our common orthography has very frequently the sound of *z ;* and in these cases must, of course, be written in Tachygraphy by the letter ⌒.

48. The sound (has no corresponding letter in the old alphabet. This sound is represented by *z* in the word *azure,* and by *s* in the words *pleasure, measure, treasure,* &c. It is, however, a simple elementary sound, and deserves a simple and appropriate letter.

49. The sound (is usually written with the common digraph *sh,* as in *show;* but it is also written with the letters *ti* and *ci*, as in *nation, Grecian,* &c.

50. The letters ⟍ and ⟍ stand for the old *th* as heard in *then* and *thin*. The heavy sound in *then* differs from the light sound in *thin,* as *d* differs from *t*. The student should be careful to distinguish these two sounds of *th*, and to employ ⟍ when the sound is vocal, and ⟍ when it is aspirate.

THE LIQUIDS AND ING.

51. The letters ⌒ ⌣ ⌣ ⌐ and ⁄ are not arranged in pairs, as the preceding letters have been. They are all vocal, and might properly have been represented by heavy curves; but being letters of frequent occurrence, having no lighter correlative sounds, it is much more convenient to represent them as given in the alphabet.

Ing. ⌣ differs from ⌣ in sound radically, instead of being a mere variety of the same sound, as other letters so paired are.

52. *Wa* and *ya*. The letters ⁄ and ⌐ have a very feeble consonantal power, and, occurring always in the

commencement of a syllable, the forms given (always written upwards) are very convenient. They have no correlative sounds.

53. The letters ⌒ and ⌒ represent sounds that are considered diphthongal; ⌒ being composed of the sounds — and ([⌒], and ⌒ of the sounds — and ([⌒].

THE DIRECTION IN WHICH THE LETTERS ARE WRITTEN.

54. The letters | | \ \ )) ((⌒ and ⌒ are invariably struck downwards, and may be called *descenders*.

The letters — — ⌒ ⌒ ⌣ ⌣ ⌐ and ⌐ are written from left to right, and may be called *horizontals*.

The letters ⁄ ⌒ and ⁄ are invariably written upwards, and may be called *ascenders*.

VARIABLE LETTERS.

The letters ⌒ ⌒ and ⁄ may be written either upward or downward, and may be called the *variable letters*. Written upward, they are named *Ma*, *La*, and *Ra;* written downward, *Em*, *El*, and *Ar*, respectively.

55. The letters ⌒ and ⌒ may be reversed into ⌐ and ⌐, when they thus form a more convenient angle with the letters to which they are joined in writing.

Note.—In a universal alphabet, the last forms are needed to represent other sounds; but, as most of the writers of the art use only the English language, it is considered allowable to turn these forms to service in the common and reporting styles of Tachygraphy, leaving those who cultivate a literary style, for use in foreign languages, to appropriate them to other sounds.

SIZE OF THE LETTERS.

Writing Exercise.

Tha,
Tha,
M,
N,
Ng,
L,
Ra,
Ar,
Wa,
Ya,
Ha,
Ja,
Cha,

SIZE OF THE LETTERS.

56. The consonant letters should be made by the student, when commencing the practice of the art, about one-sixth of an inch; but, after he has become skilful in its use, he may reduce their size to about one-eighth of an inch. The speed of the writing is increased by lessening the size of the letters.

VOCAL SIGNS.

57. The student should practise on the vocal signs in the same manner as he is instructed, in the preceding section, to practise on the consonantals.

58. The semicircles ⌒ ⌒ ⌣ and ⌣ are determined by the direction in which they are struck, rather than by the

form which they assume when written. The first pair (⌒ and ⌒) are always struck in the direction in which the hands of a watch move; but they may turn round toward the right as far as may be necessary to form a proper angle with the following letter.

ILLUSTRATION.

The second pair (⌣ and ⌣) may turn in the opposite direction, as follows:—

These forms become perfectly definite when joined to other letters, as they always must be if varied. The freedom and beauty of the writing is greatly increased by the power to vary these letters as shown above.

59. The letters ɩ and ͺ are variable in direction, being struck either in the direction of ＼ or |, as may be most convenient.

Exercise.

ɩ＼ɩ＼ɩ＼   ɩ＼ɩ＼ɩ＼   ɩ＼ɩ＼   ɩ＼ɩ＼

60. The letter ╱ is struck downward in most cases; but it may be written upward when more convenient. This sign [╱] is made light to represent the sound heard in the words *or, nor,* &c.

61. The letter ╱ (*o* short) always represents the vocal sound heard in *on, odd,* &c., and is distinguished from the light sign given in paragraph 60, by being nearly always struck upward. It is also written at a greater inclination.

SIZE OF THE VOCAL SIGNS.

62. The vocal signs should be about one-fifth the size of the consonant signs. This will make the semicircles about one-thirtieth of an inch in diameter, and the dashes one-thirtieth of an inch in length.

Exercise.

Downward, / / /   / / /   / / / / /   / / /   / / /
Upward, / / / /   / /   / /   / / / /   / /   / /
Oi and ow, ⌄ ⌄ ⌄ ⌄   ᴧ ᴧ ᴧ ᴧ ⌄ ⌄ ⌄ ⌄   ᴧ   ᴧ ⌄   ⌄
I and u, ⌄ ⌄ ⌄ ⌄ᴧ ᴧ ᴧ ᴧ ⌄ ⌄ ⌄ ⌄ᴧ ᴧ ᴧ⌄ ⌄ ⌄

CHAPTER V.

METHOD OF JOINING THE LETTERS.

63. Having memorized the letters of the alphabet, by frequently repeating the exercises given in the preceding chapter, the student should now proceed to join the letters into short syllables, or words of two letters. All letters are joined in the simplest manner. It is only necessary to observe the principles already given as to the proper direction of the letters, and the amount of variation allowed in certain vowels.

All silent letters that appear in the common print are omitted in Tachygraphy; and the true phonetic equivalents are used in place of the common orthography.

CONNECTING THE SIGNS. 51

Examples.

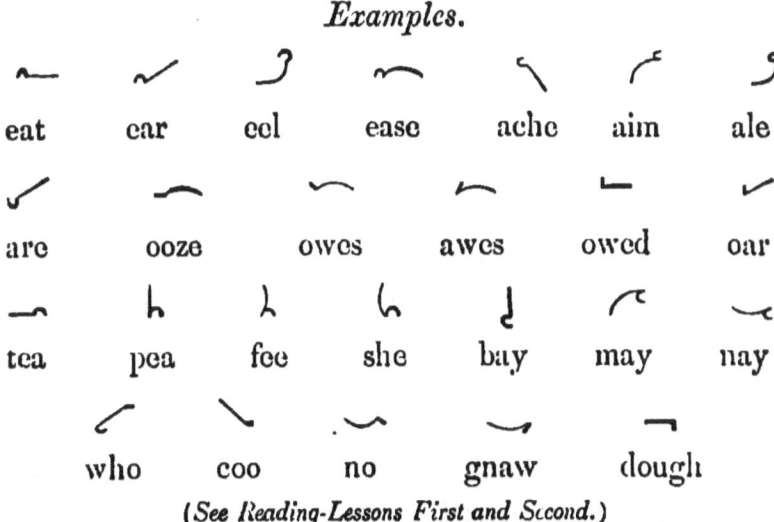

(*See Reading-Lessons First and Second.*)

64. The principles of joining apply, with some specific differences, to the various classes of vocals; hence we treat of connecting the *semicircles*, the *dashes*, and the *diamond points*, under special rules.

CONNECTING THE SEMICIRCLES.

65. The semicircles must always form an angle with the following consonant; hence ⌒ ⌒ ᴗ and ᴗ are varied, as explained in paragraph 58; but there is no need of an angle when the semicircle is joined to the end of the strokes: they form hooks in such cases, as will be seen in the examples below.

CONNECTING THE DASH-LETTERS.

66. The dashes always make angles with the preceding letters, as well as with those that follow.

67. The horizontal dashes - and · admit of no variation. When they do not make a distinct angle

with the letter or letters to which they belong, they are disjoined, and treated as non-connectives. (See paragraphs 87–92.)

68. The ׀ and ╲ take either the direction of | or ╲; that direction always being chosen which makes the acutest angle. When they form no angle in either of these directions, or when between two other letters they fail to join properly with either, they are also disjoined.

69. The dash ╱ is struck upward when it makes a better angle; but it should be struck downward whenever it is at all convenient. The light dash ╱, though struck upward generally, may be struck downward when necessary to form a good angle.

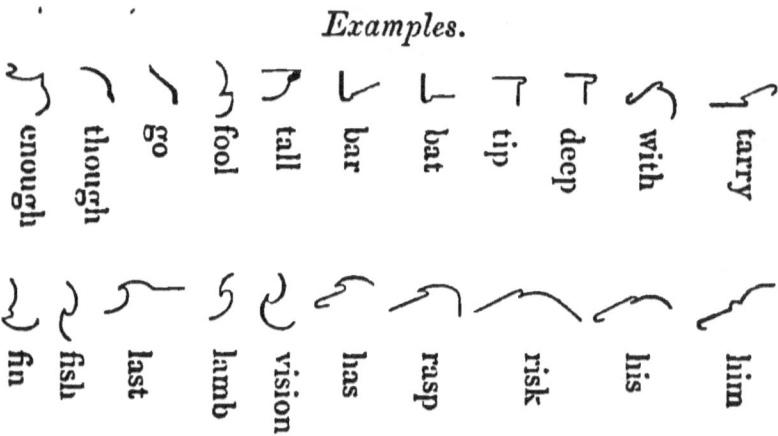

Examples.

THE DIAMOND POINTS.

70. The letters ᴠ and ᴧ may be formed of lines curving outward, when they will thus connect more easily with either a preceding or a following consonant. Either the first stroke or the second may be curved, or both strokes; or both may be made straight, as in the alphabet.

JOINING FULL-SIZED LETTERS. 53

No rule need be given in reference to the use of these letters, except that, generally, that form is best that makes the most distinct angle with the letter to which it is joined.

71. The light strokes of the letters ⌒ and ⌒ may be curved in a similar manner; and even the heavy strokes may be slightly curved in a few cases.

Examples.

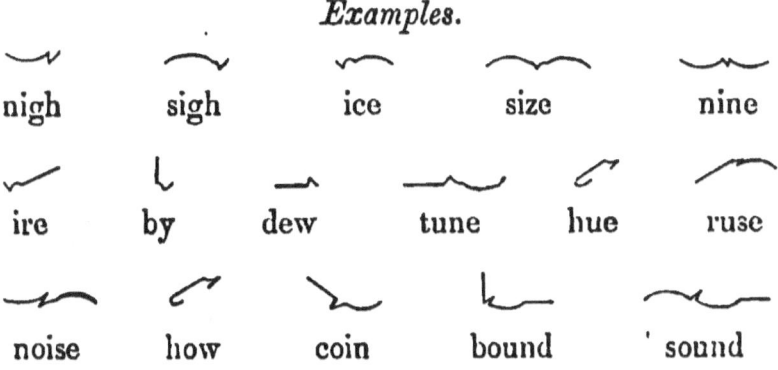

nigh   sigh   ice   size   nine

ire   by   dew   tune   hue   ruse

noise   how   coin   bound   sound

NOTE.—Before proceeding to the next section, the student should attend carefully to Reading-Lessons Third, Fifth, and Sixth.

THE JOINING OF FULL-SIZED LETTERS.

72. The consonantal *strokes* and *curves*, when joined without intervening vocals, make angles of a determinate mathematical quantity, in accordance with the principles of geometry. They sometimes unite without angles; and this, too, is to be determined by fixed mathematical laws.

ANGLES.

73. The angles formed by uniting the right lines of the alphabet may vary in quantity from 30 degrees to

135 degrees. But it will be sufficient for the practice of the art to class them as *right*, *acute*, or *obtuse* angles.

Examples.

Right angles,
A cute "
Obtuse "

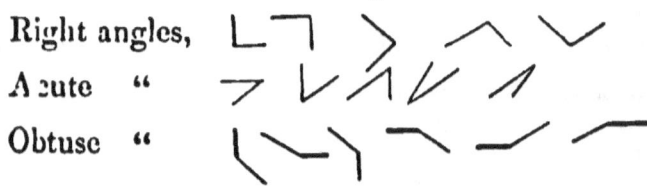

Note. \/ and /\ are classed among the right angles, although the angle is greater than 90 degrees.

RIGHT LINES JOINED WITH CURVES.

74. When straight and curved lines join, the angle cannot be preserved in many cases where mathematical accuracy would require one.

75. When the curve faces the angle, and would, if straight, form an obtuse angle with the right line, no angle can be formed; for the right line would form a tangent to the curve.

Examples.

76. When the curve, situated as above, is in such a direction as would make, if straight, a right angle, the angle is sacrificed for convenience in writing.

Examples.

77. And even in cases where the curve faces an angle that would be acute if formed of right lines, the

angle is often rounded so much, that the two letters unite into one stroke.

Examples.

THE JOINING OF CURVES.

78. Facing curves, of such a direction that their chords would form right angles, always form half-circles.

Examples.

79. Facing curves whose chords would form acute angles are joined without angles.

Examples.

80. But facing curves whose chords would form obtuse angles must in all cases form an angle.

Examples.

OPPOSING CURVES.

81. Opposing curves *in the same direction* unite into a waved line.

Examples.

56   VOCALS JOINED WITH VOCALS.

82. Opposing curves in different directions always make angles.

Examples.

CURVES REPEATED.

83. When the same curve is repeated, an angle is formed.

Examples.

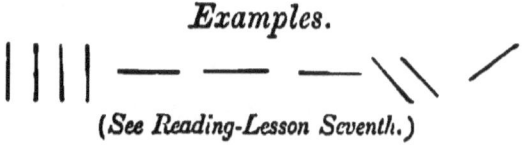

STRAIGHT LINES REPEATED.

84. Two right lines in the same direction unite without an angle. If one of the lines is heavy, and the other light, the shading should be so gradual that both letters may blend into one stroke.

Examples.

| | | | | — — — \\\\ /

(*See Reading-Lesson Seventh.*)

VOCALS JOINED WITH VOCALS.

85. The principles explained in the previous part of this chapter apply, for the most part, to the connection of vocals with vocals. It should be observed, however, that the vocal curves are *half-circles,* and unite with different angles from those formed by quarter-circles similarly situated.

86. The *dashes* make the same angles as full-sized strokes similarly situated. They cannot unite with other

DISJOINED VOCALS. 57

dashes without an angle, but may take a vowel-hook, as full-sized letters do.

Examples.

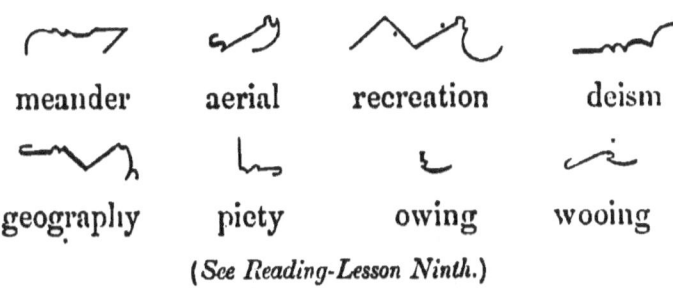

meander   aerial   recreation   deism

geography   piety   owing   wooing

(*See Reading-Lesson Ninth.*)

DISJOINED VOCALS.

87. The *dots* are always disjoined; the *dashes* are disjoined in many instances; and the *semicircles* in a few cases. A disjoined vocal is written near to some full-sized letter in the syllable to which it belongs, and has a position with reference to that letter.

88. If the vocal is to be read before a perpendicular or inclined stroke, it is written on the left of it; if read after, on the right.

89. If the vocal is read before a horizontal stroke, it is written above it; if after, below it.

90. When the disjoined vocal occurs between two full-sized letters which belong to the same syllable, it is generally written with the latter, except as provided in the next section.

91. The *dots* are written near the middle of the letter; and, when they occur between two letters, the heavy *dot* is written with the former, and the light *dot* with the latter.

OTHER DISJOINED VOCALS.

Examples.

ebb egg air rare faith feather web keg debt bury

Edit do etch chair soul

foot come known far face nonentity

92. Other disjoined vocals may be written near the beginning, middle, or end of the letter; but, if the vocal is written last, it will generally be more convenient to write it near the end of the latter of the two strokes between which it occurs.

93. If the word contains more than one syllable, it is better to write the vowel with that consonant to which it belongs in pronouncing the word.

94. When there are three or more consonants, the vocals must, of course, be written in their proper syllables, not in connection with letters from which they are separated in speech. (See the examples in paragraph 91.)

THE CONNECTING STROKE.

95. When the *semicircles* do not join conveniently, it is often better to connect them in the outline by means of a slight stroke than to disjoin them.

This stroke should be light, and briefer than the vowel strokes. It may be in any direction, but should be written generally perpendicular to the letters which it joins.

If the *semicircle* occurs between two full strokes, to neither of which it will join without a connecting stroke, it is better to disjoin it.

Examples.

aid   fade   each   reach   knee   purvey

NOTE. — *No connecting stroke is used with the dashes or diamond points.*

The use of this stroke is very infrequent, and it may be avoided in all cases by disjoining the vocals when it would be required; but in such words as *aid, paid, made,* &c., its use adds to the facility of writing by giving continuity, and it also increases the gracefulness of the outlines. There seems to be some reason for joining an initial vowel, which does not apply with so much force to a medial vowel. A disjoined vocal in *aid* and *each* does not look as well as in *fade* and *reach.* One reason for this is the case with which a medial vowel may be spared in reading. The eye is arrested by the first letters of a word, and passes more lightly over the remaining letters, if the form of the word is plain enough to be understood.

(*See Reading-Lessons Third and Eighth.*)

CHAPTER VI.

THE METHOD OF STUDY.

96. WHEN the student of the art has mastered the theory given in the preceding chapter, he should turn his attention to the practice of the principles learned.

And, to make his practice productive of any good results, he must have a definite plan, and follow it.

Skill in reading should keep pace with skill in writing. The student should read, in connection with his study and practice of this chapter, the *first nine* Reading-Exercises in the end of the book. They should be reviewed until they can be read as easily as the common print; and the forms there given should be consulted in all cases of difficulty in combination. In addition to this, the student should read his own exercises, and write nothing that he is unable to read. Skill in writing must be based on a knowledge of the *principles* of the art. These can be acquired practically only by special *drill* on each principle by itself. This *drill* should be made to accomplish two purposes: 1st, To render the method of combining the characters more familiar; and, 2d, To train the hand to skill in forming the word-forms.

No one plan can be exhaustive; but the following will be found to yield good results if faithfully followed.

97. Let the alphabet be so thoroughly mastered, that all the characters can be written within fifteen or twenty seconds. For the method of practice, see Chapter IV. When every sound in a word instantly suggests its appropriate letter, the first point is gained; then the student should proceed to gain the greatest facility in joining the letters.

To accomplish this, let him write each vocal before every consonantal in the alphabet, except *wa*, *ya*, and *ha*, as follows:—

THE METHOD OF PRACTICE. 61

[shorthand characters]

This should be repeated until perfectly familiar to the eye, and until the fingers can execute it with perfect facility and a tolerable degree of accuracy. When mastered sufficiently, the preceding exercise can be written within fifteen seconds.

Then proceed with the next vocal in the same manner, adding every consonantal, except *wa*, *ya*, and *ha*, which are not so frequently preceded by vowels as the regular consonants; and in the same manner join all the vocals to the *following* consonants, or disjoin them, as the case may be.

98. When this is thoroughly mastered, join all the vocals to preceding consonants, omitting the signs of the short vowels, which are never final.

Examples.

[shorthand characters]

Go through, in this way, with all the consonantals, adding all the long and diphthongal signs to each of them, and rewrite it until it is perfectly familiar.

99. The third step in this practice will be to insert all the vowels between every possible combination of the consonants. But since but a small part of the possible combinations actually occurs in writing, it will be sufficient to insert all the short vowels between every consonant, as follows: —

[shorthand characters]

In connection with this practice, read the first nine Reading-Lessons, near the end of the book.

WRITING-EXERCISES.

100. It is desirable that the student should distinguish between the true sounds — the phonetic elements — in a word, and the letters employed in the common spelling. To make this easier, and to mark the pronunciation of syllables left indeterminate in the ordinary spelling, a few of the first exercises are printed by limiting the sounds of some of the old letters, and inverting or marking others, as follows : —

101. The vowels *a, e, i, o,* and *u*, retain their short sounds, as heard in *at, ebb, it, on,* and *put* (oo in *foot*) ; and the long sounds corresponding are marked by the acute accent, thus : —

fár, fét, fít, fót, fúd.
far, fate, feet, fought, food.

The *o* in *note* is marked *ó;* the *u* in *up, ú;* and the long sound of *i* and *u* by the digraphs *ei* and *iu;* thus : —

nót, nút, neit, niuz.
note, nut, night, news.

102. The sound of *th* heard in the word *that* is represented by an inverted D ; thus, ⸺ : the sharper sound, heard in *thin,* is written in the usual way. The letter *c* is omitted, *s* being used for it when soft, and *k* when hard ; *z* is written for *s* when the sound of *z* occurs ; *j* is written for *g* soft; and *g* always retains its hard sound, heard in *go.*

The sound of *z* in *azure* has no proper representative

in the common print: it is here designated by the letter *j* with the lower part slightly clipped.

Examples.

kùm,	rúj,	shō,	íz.
come,	rouge,	show,	ease.
ȼem,	thùm,	éj,	ék.
them,	thumb,	age,	ache.

NOTE. — The above scheme is taken, in part, from the Kosmic alphabet of the American Philological Society, Rev. N. Brown, 37 Park Row, New York, president. We have, however, adopted only such distinctive signs as seemed absolutely necessary to express the sounds intended in an intelligible manner. Those desiring to secure a more perfect phonetic scheme should procure the Kosmic alphabet, which is extensively employed by foreign missionaries in printing uncultivated languages.

EXERCISE FIRST.

To be written in Tachygraphic characters, for correction by the teacher. It will be well to leave two lines blank under every line written, so that, after the exercise has been corrected on the second line, it can be rewritten by the pupil on the third.

Long Vowels.

E long: íb, íp, íg, ík, íd, ít, ív, íf, íz, ís, íȼ, íth, ím, ín, íng, íl, ír, íj, ích. (See examples in paragraph 97.)

A long: éb, ép, ég, ék, éd, ét, év, éf, éj, ésh, éz, és, éȼ, éth, ém, én, él, éj, éch.

NOTE. — The third vocal, *á*, occurs seldom before any other letter than *r*, and may be omitted in these exercises.

Oo long: úb, úp, úg, úk, úd, út, úv, úf, új, úsh, úz, ús, úȼ, úth, úm, ún, úng, úl, úr, új, úch.

O long: ōb, ōp, ōg, ōk, ōd, ōt, ōv, ōf, ōj, ōsh, ōz, ōs, ōȼ, ōth, ōm, ōn, ōng, ōl, ōr, ōj, ōch.

WRITING EXERCISES.

Au (as in *taught*) : *ób, óp, óg, ók, ód, ót, óv, óf, ój, ósh, óz, ós, óm, ón, ong, ól, ór.*

EXERCISE SECOND.
Short Vowels.

I short : *ib, ip, ig, ik, id, it, iv, if, ij, ish, iz, is, iſ, ih, im, in, ing, il, ir.*

E short : *eb, ep, eg, ek,* &c., through all the consonants.

A short : *ab, ap, ag, ak,* &c., as above.

Oo short (as in *foot*), *ub, up, ug, uk,* &c.

U short (as in *up*), *ŭb, ŭp, ŭg, ŭk,* &c.

O short (as in *on*), *ob, op, og, ok,* &c.

EXERCISE THIRD.
Vocals joined to Preceding Consonants.

B : *bí, bé, bá, bú, bō, bó. P* : *pí, pé, pá, pú, pō, pó.*

Go on in this way, adding all the long vowels to every consonant in the Tachygraphic alphabet, except *ing*.

EXERCISE FOURTH.
The joining of the Diphthongal Signs.

I long : *bei* (by), *pei* (pie), *gei, kei, dei, tei, vei, fei, jei, shei, zei, sei, ɑei, thei, mei, nei, lei, rei, wei, yei, hei, jei, chei.*

U long : *biu, piu* (pew), *giu, kiu, diu, tiu,* &c., throughout the alphabet.

Oi : *boi, poi, goi, koi* (coy), *doi, toi,* &c., as above.

Ou : *bou* (bow or bough), *pou, gou, kou* (cow), *dou, tou,* &c.

EXERCISE FIFTH.

Eib, iub, oib, oub, eip, iup, oip, oup, eig, iug, oig, oug, &c., through the whole alphabet, omitting the letters *wa, ya,* and *ha.*

WRITING EXERCISES.

EXERCISE SIXTH.

Ib, eb, ab, ub, ŭb, ob, ip, ep, ap, up, ŭp, op, &c., through the alphabet, as above.

EXERCISE SEVENTH.

Bib, big, bid, bif, bish, bis, bith, bim, bin, bil, bir.
Kip, kik, kit, kif, kish, kiss, kith, kim, kin, king, kill, kir.
Tip, tik, tit, tif, tish, tis, tith, tim, tin, ting, til, tir.
Fip, fik, fit, fif, fish, fith, fim, fin, fing, fil, fir.
Sip, sik, sit, sif, sis, sim, sin, sil, ŝir, sing.
Mip, mik, mit, mif, mish, mis, mith, mim, min, ming, mil, mir.
Nip, nik, nit, nif, nis, nith, nim, nin, nil, nir.
Lip, lik, lit, liv, lis, lith, lim, lin, ling, lil, lir, lich, lij.
Rip, rik, rid, riv, ris, rith, rim, rin, ring, ril, rich, rij.
Wip, wik, wit, wif, wish, wis, with, wim, win, wing, wil, wich.
Hip, hik, hid, hif, his, hith, him, hin, hing, hil, hich.
Chip, chik, chid, chif, chis, chim, chin, chil.

EXERCISE EIGHTH.

Beb, beg, bed, bev, bes, beth, bem, ben, bel, ber, geb, geg, ged, gev, ges, gem, gen, gel, ger, &c., commencing with the letters *d, v, z, m, n, l, r, w, h,* and *j,* and using all the short vowels *a, u, ŭ,* and *o.*

EXERCISE NINTH.
Consonants united without Vowels.

Bk, bt, br (*ra*), *pg, pd, pr, gk, gd, gr, db, dk, dr* (*ar*), *rr, rp, rk, rt, wp, wk, wd, wr, hb, hg, hd, hr.*
Btha, ptha, gn, kn, dth, tth, rs, rz, wz, sg, sk, shg, shk, md, mt, mr (*ra*).
Bn, pn, bng, png, dv, df, tv, tf, kl, gl, sb, sp, mg, mk, mb, mp, dl, tl, bl, pl, rv, rf, rl.
Shtha, sh☾a, thn, ☾n, zth, ☾z, thf, thv, ms, mz, nl, nyl.
Jz, js, shz, shs, vn, vng, fn, fng, zsh, ssh, mn, mng, nf, nv.

EXERCISE TENTH.

Bb, bp, gg, gk, dd, dt, pb, pp, kg, kk, td, tt, jn, jng, shn, shng, zv, zf, sv, sf, ɖ ala, thala, mɖ, mth, jla, shla, mv, mf, ml, zl, sl, zn, sn, zng, sng, ml, la-m, vsh, fsh, ththa, tha-th.
Ii, ié, id, iú, iō, ió. Ii, ie, ia, iu, iů, io, iei, iiu, ioi, iou, ii, éi, ái, ńi, ōi, ói, eii, ńi, oii, oui.

NOTE. — The preceding exercises will be found to comprise nearly all the combinations of the Tachygraphic letters which occur in writing the English language. The student can master these combinations in no other way so well as to rewrite these exercises until they are perfectly familiar. Negligence in this part of the work will add to the labor of mastering the art. They must be familiarized in some way. The negligent student, who prefers to master each combination as he meets it in writing, will continue to blunder for months; while the diligent pupil, who masters these combinations here, will find that no real difficulties can occur in his subsequent writing.

EXERCISE ELEVENTH.

Spelled in the common orthography. The silent letters should be omitted.

Pea, bee, eat. Ape, pay, bay, day. Key, eke, gay, ache, too, dough, toe, oat, aught, cow, dow.
Tea, day, thee, they, see, say, saw, awes, owes, ooze. She, show, shaw, foe, oaf, oath. Are, say, me, may, ma, aim, nay, know, gnaw. Hay, ho, haw. Way, woe, we. You, who. Lea, law, low. Eel, awl, ale, oar, mow.
It, cat, at, are, age, odd, awed, of, off, the, thee, us, owes, is, case, easy, allay, an, Anna.
Tie, die, toy, joy, coy. Bow, vow, cow, out, owl, oil. Nigh, dew, view, few, mew, cue. Die, due, cow, cue, coy, tie, toy, high, hoy, my, mew, mow (ou), wry, right, wine, wind, coin. About, gout, annoy, duty, night, nine, might, mine, tight, tipe, foul, thou.

WRITING EXERCISES.

Ice, eyes, dice, ties, nice, rise, vice, vies. Hew, new, news, liew, rue. How, now, allow. Sigh, sighs, sign. Royce, toys, noise.
Go up nigh. Now see how it is! Is ease the aim? How may we find the right way? This is the right way. May we walk now, or by and by? You may go now.

EXERCISE TWELFTH.

Ebb, egg, etch, edge. Err, air, fir, fair, bird, bare, were, wear. Very, ferry, merry, mercy. To, do, so. Good, food, mood, could, would, should. Not, but, tub, knob, notch.
Do they err if they do so? They may do so. It is easy to do it. Is it so easy? We may know more about this by and by. How do you know this? I know the way, and have often seen the view you mention.
Said, led, wed, head. There, care, rare. Wreck, web, men, ten, then, aired.
If he said so, then you may act on it. We now know how you and they were led to do this. There is no other way so good. You may attain this if you desire to do so. The good and wise are often led by a way they know not.
Ope, open, rope, robe, though, pope, poet, poem. Love, enough, tough, govern. Undone, unwise, uncle, unworthy (onward). Up, ut, us, hum.
Bone, cone, tone, moan, port, import. They have done so, and we may hope to do the same. The vessel is not yet in port. The import of his answer is this.

EXERCISE THIRTEENTH.

In, bin, fin. As, ask. Epistle, epoch. Aid, paid, bade. Dish, ye, knee, each, teach.
Faith, fade, fasten, separate, nourish, cherish, tuition.
Cat, bat, jack, jacket, bad, pad. Tick, wick. Thin, king, give, gift, forgive, arithmetic. Shall, shanty, shad.

His, has, list, last, mist, mast, wist, rasp, hist, hast. Fact, fancy, than.

Deed, did,* heal, hill, weal, will, meal, mill, seal, till, reel, ril, wreak, rick, reed, rid, heed, hid, heat, hit, weed, wit, wisdom, seen, sin, keen, kin.

Deep, dip,* reap, rip, weep, weak, wick, leak. Barrel, bar,* parrot, part, garret, guard, carry, car, tarry, tar.

He did the deed.* They paid for the fish. If ye had faith as a grain of mustard-seed, ye should say to this mountain, Be ye removed, and be ye cast into the sea, and it should obey you.

Beat, bet, pate, pat, pet. Beak, pick, beck, big, beg, peg. Lack, talk, nook. Dip, top, nap, sack, tack. Dog, dig, dim, tame, dumb, numb. Came, game, name, same.

Keg, dead, debt, edged, etched, jet, caged, dated. Edited, noted.

Gig, cake, deed, did, cog, pip, pop, publish, baptism, judgment.

Non, says, cease, unended, nonentity, fifty, five, thither.

Shovel, sheaf, fish. Sometimes, seldom, sold. Sun, notion, mission, sadness, send, occasion.

Nonsensical, business, Johnson, lemon, insufficiency, inefficiency, insincere, multitude, darkness.

* NOTE.—The long vowel in *deed* is distinguished from the short vowel in *did* by writing the former in the full form, and using the hook for the latter. The ⌒ is distinguished from the ⌒ in this way wherever convenient; but, in other cases, the hook is made larger for the long vowel than for the short. The same principle applies to the letters ◡ and ◡; the hook being larger when written for ◡ than when written for ◡.

(See *Reading-Lessons*, paragraphs 33, 37, and 38.)

EXERCISE FOURTEENTH.

Iota, Iowa, curious, geology, geography, individual. Deist, theism, being, seing, owing, knowing, viewing, allowing, alliance.

Idea, Indiana, meridian, meander, serial, really, aerial, ideality.
Saying, conveying, allaying, creation, arraying.
Doing, wooing, cooing, Louis.
Science, scientific, vowel, avowal, dual.
Society, variety, piety, sighing, renewal.
The science of geology unfolds many curiosities. Geography is a science of much value, conveying a knowledge of all states of society, with all the various customs of different nations. An aerial voyage must give delightful views of landscape scenery. Individuals materially augment their importance by advantageous alliances. Ideality and materiality are really quite various in conceptions of spirituality.

CHAPTER VII.

CONSONANTAL DIPHTHONGS.

103. ALL the words in the language may be written in accordance with the principles explained in the preceding chapters. It is very desirable to avoid all unnecessary complication; and the art could doubtless be rendered serviceable, to some extent, without adding any new principles. As we have already signs for all the sounds in the language, it would be unphonetic to add other signs to represent these sounds as simple elements, and it would, besides, lead to great perplexity in their use. Nothing further would be needed in theory, or tolerable in practice, if some sounds were not blended together, and uttered with one impulse of the voice. Some of these diphthongal sounds are composed of *l* or

r, preceded by a stronger letter, *b*, *p*, *g*, *k*, &c., as in *pry*, *play*, *glow*, *grow*, &c. The letters *pr*, *pl*, *gr*, and *gl*, are uttered with one impulse of the voice.

Another class are composed of *s*, followed by *p*, *k*, *t*, *f*, *m*, *n*, *l*, and *w*, as in the words *spy*, *sky*, *stay*, &c. To these may be added the sound of *wh*, as heard in *why*.

104. It adds both to the rapidity and to the legibility of the writing to give these diphthongal combinations distinctive signs. This becomes more important in hurried writing, where obscure vowels are omitted; for it enables the reader to determine instantly a word that might otherwise be indefinite.

REMARK. — The representation of two consonant sounds by one letter is not at all new in language. The ancient Greeks had the double letters *stigma* and *psi*, the German has *zet* (tset), and in Latin and English we have *x*; all *of* which letters represent combinations less important than those of the *l*, *r*, and *s* series given below.

105. It is convenient both in theory and practice to distinguish between the use of these compounds in the commencement, and their use in the end, of syllables. They are more perfectly diphthongal in the first case, and it is more important that they should be properly distinguished.

So all compounds are divided into two classes, — the *initial* and the *final*. All of those called *initial* occur also as final; but the final compounds are not all initial. We treat first of the class of

INITIAL COMPOUNDS.

106. The *l*-series initial are *bl*, *pl*, *gl*, *kl*, and *fl;* the *r*-series initial, *br*, *pr*, *gr*, *kr*, *dr*, *tr*, *fr*, *thr*, and *shr*.

INITIAL COMPOUNDS.

They are represented by modifying the signs already known, as follows: —

bl, pl, gl, kl, fl, br, pr, gr, kr, dr, tr, fr, thr, shr.

It will be noticed that the hook is on the right for the *l*-series, and on the left for the *r*-series. It is inconvenient to write a hook on the back side of a curved letter; hence the ⟩ is hooked for *fl*, instead of the ⟩. So also ⟋ is hooked for *shr* instead of (. The letters ⟩ and ⟩ should be noted as irregular, and will need especial attention in practice.

107. The *s*-series initial are the following: —

sp, sk, st, sf, sm, sn, sl, sw.

It will be noticed that the circle is on the right side of | and \, on the upper side of — and ⟋, and on the inside of the curves. When these signs occur in the middle of a word, special rules are observed as follows: —

Case 1. — Between two straight letters in the same direction, the circle retains its original position.

Case 2. — Between straight letters that make an angle, it is always on the outside of the angle, as ⌐ bestow, ⌐ obscure.

Case 3. — Between a straight and a curved line, the circle is always on the inside of the curve. (See Reading-Lessons, paragraph 67.)

When ⟋ is medial, the hook of the ⟋ appears.

108. The letter *s* precedes the diphthongal sounds of the *l* and *r* series in a few cases, forming triphthongs.

They are the following: —

⌐ ⌐ ⌒ and ⌒
spl, spr, scr,   *str.*

REMARK 1. — In the case given above, where *three* letters unite, as in the words *spread, street,* &c., it would seem as proper to consider the *sp* the diphthong as the *pr;* but the forms given above are the most convenient. The ⌒ joins to preceding letters more conveniently than the circle would do. In all cases where the *s*-series is followed by the *l* or *r* series, it yields to them, and the *s* is written in its alphabetic form.

REMARK 2. — The circle should not be made inside of the hook, as it is in Phonography. The fuller forms are more convenient and facile.

REMARK 3. — When *s* is preceded by a vowel in the commencement of a word, the long sign is used, except in a few cases after the letter ʋ.

DIRECTIONS FOR PRACTICE.

1. Read Exercises Ten and Eleven in the end of the book. 2. Drill on the compounds of the *l* and *r* series until you are as familiar with them as with the alphabet. 3. Write the following.

EXERCISE FIFTEENTH.

Bl, pl, gl, kl, fl. Blow, play, plow, glow, clew, clay, claim, gleam, blame, disclaim, emblazon, enclose, displace, flow, fled, influx, reclaim, declaim, reply, apply, application.

Br, pr, gr, kr, dr, tr, fr, thr, shr. Brow, brown, brain, breeze. Preach, principle, proper, pretences. Great, greatness, gravity, grievance. Crown, creep, crockery. Drive, trial, trivial. Frame, from. Three. Shrewd. Apprehend, April.

In the beginning, God created the heavens and the earth. Greatness and glory shall crown the achievement. Truth crushed to earth shall rise again. That shrewd and thriving man of business gives freely for every improvement. Though his powers of comprehension were not considered very brilliant, yet he apprehended our design with little explanation.

4. Drill on the characters of the *s*-series, and write —

EXERCISE SIXTEENTH.

Sp, st, sk, sf, sm, sn, sl, sw. Spare, spoil, speak. Stay, stand, stiff. Sky, sketch, skiff. Sphere, spherical, sphinx. Small, smite, smith. Snow, sneer. Slough, slim. Sweep, swear.
Inspiration, instances, insphere, ensnare, enslave, unswerving. Espy, estate, escape, hemisphere, dismiss, dislocate.

Give especial attention to small things. Observe the *s* in *sphere* and *hemisphere*, in *escape* and *landscape*, in *state* and *estate*, in *spy* and *espy*, &c.

Spr, skr, str, spl. Spray, spread, spring. Screen, scroll, scribble. Stray, street, strive. Splendor, resplendent, explain. Sapple, sickle, sicker, supper, sadder, suitor. Stir, spear, scare, spool, frown. Spring, screen, splint, scrawl, stick, stake, speak, streak, strike, smoke, destroy, distress, prosper, express, describe, descry, subscribe, disgrace, disclaim, discreet, exclaim, disclaimer, discriminate, disagree.

QU, AND THE COMPOUNDS WITH W.

109. The digraph *wh* represents a very close diphthong, if, indeed, it may not properly be considered a simple sound. It has for its first element the sound of *h*, and for the second a whispered sound of *w*, not heard in English, except in combination. The second sound in the diphthong *qu* is the same; and, when ⟋ is used for this sound, it should be noticed that this letter has, in this combination, a less vocal sound than when it is initial.

The combinations *tw*, *thw*, *dw*, and *gw*, end with the same sound, except that, when *w* is preceded by *d* and *g*, it partakes in a measure of the vocality of these letters; but when combined with *q*, *t*, and *h*, it is assimilated to them, and becomes a whispered sound.

110. We have given only one distinctive sign for these combinations; *wha*, written ⁄, differing from ⁄ in one respect only. The hook of the *wha* is heavier.

The others are written as follows:—

gw,   qu,   dw,   tw,   thw.

EXERCISE SEVENTEENTH.

Why, while, where, wherein, wherever, wherefore, which, wharf, whale, wheel, whiff, whip, whelm, when, whence, whenever, whensoever, wheresoever, whereas, whereat, whereinto, whereof, whereon, whirl, whisper.

Quick, quiet, quarrel, quench, quill, quail, quart, query, quarry, qualify, quality, quantity, quarto, querulous, quickness, quiesce, quietism, quietly, quietness, quietude, quo animo, quota, quoth, quo warranto.

Equal, aqueous, equality, equiform, equiformity, equip, equipage, acquire, acquiring, equity, acquiesce, aqueduct, squeak, squeamish, squeeze, sway.

Dwell, dwarf, twit, twist, language, thwart.

FINAL COMPOUNDS.

111. The compounds of the *l*, *r*, and *s* series occur in the end of syllables as well as at their commencement. Though less perfectly diphthongal in this case than when initial, it is convenient in many cases to use them, since they are already memorized.

FINAL COMPOUNDS.

All the compounds of the *l* and *r* series, given as initial, occur also in final syllables, and, besides these, the following: —

dl, tl, vl, nl, vr, jr, ɑr, nr.

The use of these signs in final syllables is not uniform. Their use depends entirely upon convenience. If preceded by a consonant, as in the words *member, temple, tender,* &c., their use is generally convenient, though not always. Preceded by vocals, they are to be used only when they do not interfere with vocalization.

Examples.

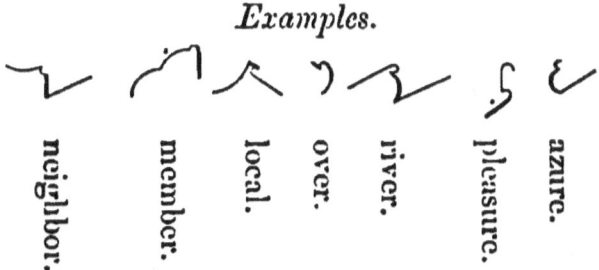

neighbor. member. local. over. river. pleasure. azure.

REMARK. — We wish to draw a strong line of demarcation between those consonant combinations that commence syllables and those that end them. Most of the former are provided with distinctive signs, as shown in the preceding section. Their use, however, is *unvaried* and *invariable*. The diphthongal sound is always represented by the diphthongal sign; hence no indefiniteness can result; and the writer can use these signs with the same freedom as the simple letters.

When, however, final compounds are introduced to represent final syllables, for example the final syllable of the word *member,* a difficulty is introduced. If all final syllables ending in *br* were written with the compound ⟩, the practice would be perfectly simple; but the word *neighbor,* for instance, is more easily written with the full form of the letters, thus:

The final syllables do not present a true diphthong. Compare the English *meter* and the French *metre*. The French pronounce the *tr* as though it commenced the syllable: we do not.

We have, then, final compounds, which we can conveniently represent by the signs of the *l, r,* and *s* series, in some cases, but which, in other cases, are not convenient. If confounded with the initial series, they would throw a degree of indefiniteness over the use of those letters, which, in their proper use, are invariable.

EXERCISE EIGHTEENTH.

Note. — The student will notice that some of the words in the second column are to be written with simple letters, and some with the diphthongal signs.

Initial Compounds.	*Final Compounds.*
pl, *employ.*	*ample.*
bl, *emblem.*	*tumble.*
kl, *incline.*	*fickle.*
gl, *glide.*	*regal.*
dl, ———.	*medal.*
tl, ———.	*metal.*
vl, ———.	*oval.*
fl, *inflame.*	*awful.*
nl, ———.	*kennel.*

R SERIES.

br, *embrace.*	*ember.*
pr, *emprize.*	*temper.*
gr, *engross.*	*anger.*
kr, *increase.*	*anchor.*
dr, *redress.*	*rudder.*
tr, *retrace.*	*writer.*
vr, ———.	*over.*
fr, *infringe.*	*suffer.*
jr, ———.	*measure.*

WRITING EXERCISES. 77

shr, *enshrine.*   *usher.*
đr, ———.   *other.*
thr, *enthrone.*   *anther.*
nr, ———.   *sooner.*

Play, pray, idle, dry, glow, grow, eagle, glee, upper, bray, tray, dray, utter, try, plow, prow, blew, brew, clew, accrue, glue, grew, tattle, latter, people, peeper, papal, paper, Babel, babber, fickle, figure, local, looker, maker, table, tabor, steeple, steeper, chapel, cheaper, trouble, drabble, trapper, trooper, broker, platter, prattle, clutter, battle, batter, flow, fro, oval, over, through, either, initial, essential, treason, pleasure, ambrosial, brother.

Treble, terrible, traitor, Tartar, frame, farm, odor, adore, utter, attire, seeker, secure, idle, dull, glow, goal, clay, coal, flow, follow, evil, volley, fritter, ferreter, break, bark, breath, birth, frail, furl, trade, tardy, blubber, pilfer, gutter, guitar, crier, currier, boulder, bladder, plaid, pallid, peal, plea, pale, play, Saturday, stride, purpose, propose, torpor, trapper, brawl, barrel, crave, carve.

Supple, supper, sable, sabre, settle, setter, sickle, sicker, struggle, streamer, scribble, scruple, distress, prosper, express, expressive, extra, exclaim, disgrace, describe, disagreeable, describer, strata, pastry, disclaim, disclose, sooner, suitor, suttle, sphere, suffer, safely, safer, sever, swivel, sparrow, spray, spar, saddle, sadly, sagely, ancestor, ancestry, impostor, imply, impolite, employ, impel, temple, temper, tamper, tempter, trample, prompter, trump, tramp, plump, shrink, shriek, scream, scrawl, improve, impress, impervious, imperial, implead, impelled.

REMARK. — Those accustomed to the license in the use of these characters which is permitted in Phonography will notice that the compound is used in Tachygraphy only when the letters unite without an intervening vowel. Though the use of these compounds in final syllables leads to some indefiniteness, the difficulty is increased many fold when these signs are used in such words as *bill, dear*, &c., where the letters are separated by full vowels. This should never be done in Tachygraphy.

THE S SERIES FINAL.

112. The sounds of *s* or *z* blend with all the letters of the alphabet, except

((⌒ ⌒ ⌣ ⌒ ⌒ ⌒ and ⌒

Since *z* only can unite with a semi-vocal, and *s* only with a whispered sound, the circle may be used for either *z* or *s*.

We use *s*, in the common spelling, for *z* in such words as *heads, bags,* &c.; and even *z* for *s* in *quartz*. Since only *z* can unite with *d* and *g*, and only *s* can unite with *t*, these sounds become definite. So we have the following compounds ending in *z :*

bz, gz, dz, vz, ᴔz, mz, nz, lz, rz.

and the following ending in *s :*

ps, ks, ts, fs, ths, ns, ls, rs.

It will be noticed that *l, n,* and *r* take either *z* or *s* after them, as in *false, falls, worse, wars, hence, hens.*

To distinguish *z* from *s* after these letters, the circle is made heavy for *z*, and light for *s*, as seen in the examples above. This is not necessary in ordinary practice, but may be done when special accuracy is desirable.

113. When *s* is preceded by *e* short (represented by the light dot), the circle may be used as though no

vowel occurred. In this case, the dot is placed near the middle of the full-sized character, to which the circle is added so that it will belong to the first consonant in such words as *test, rest,* &c.

Examples.

best,　test,　rest,　zest, impressed, lesson.

EXERCISE NINETEENTH.

Shrubs, shreds, shrugs, loaves, seems, seals, seas, hopes, hats, books, hoofs, hence, else, horse, west, crest, prest, distressed, request, carelessness. He is stern, steady, and stoical. The slow snail slides smoothly along his slippery way. Whence come wars and fightings among you? He accepts the office, and attempts by his acts to conceal his faults. For the hundredth time he spoke of lengths, breadths, widths, and depths. Amidst the mists and coldest frosts, with barest wrists and stoutest boasts, he thrusts his fists against the posts, and still insists he sees the ghosts. A storm ariseth on the sea. A model vessel is struggling amidst the war of elements, quivering and shivering, shrinking and battling like a thinking being. The merciless, racking whirlwinds, like frightful fiends, howl and moan, and send sharp, shrill shrieks through the creaking cordage, snapping the sheets and masts. The sturdy sailors stand to their tasks, and weather the severest storm of the season.

CHAPTER VIII.

THE OMISSION OF VOWELS.

114. In ordinary conversation, and even in oratorical discourse, many vowels are pronounced very obscurely. To give them their full, proper sound would be considered a needless precision, and would rather offend the ear than add to the beauty of the declamation.

These sounds embarrass the phonetician. If he writes the sounds fully, and reads accordingly, he is too pedantic. If he attempts to represent these obscure sounds in all their minute shadings, he multiplies signs to his own embarrassment, and to the utter confusion of the great multitude, who have less appreciation of the delicate shadings of the sounds of the language.

Were it our design to develop a literary style of writing, whose chief excellence was to consist in the accuracy with which it represented the sounds of the language, we should have but little hope of bringing the subject within the reach of all. But the following rules will be found extremely simple, and lead to a style of writing sufficiently accurate for all the ordinary purposes of life. If, for any purpose, it should be desirable to write any thing more accurately, all the vowels should be written fully.

The omission of a few vowels, as indicated here, cannot embarrass the reader, as it will very seldom happen that the outlines will be left equivocal.

It must be distinctly understood, that the following

rules are for the more advanced writer, and that, while the adept can dispense with all vowels that do not connect readily, the less skilful Tachygrapher will do well to write all except those that are so obscure as to be somewhat indefinite.

RULE 1. Omit all obscure vowels; as, for instance, the *o* in *mason, nation, lesson,* &c., the final *e* in *lessen, lesser, level,* &c., the *iou* in *contagious,* &c.

EXERCISE TWENTIETH.

Omit the vowels in the final syllables of the following words: —

Centre, enter, winter, fester, letter, ever, never, river, pepper, gospel, barrel, novel, coral, pastor, parlor.

Immortal, parental, triumphal, eternal, diurnal, abandon, demon, razor, major, minor, rumor, terror, mirror, censor, citron, piston, canon, dictator, testator, envelope, develop.

Anonymous, ungenerous, analogous, motion, action, unction, mansion, proposition, arithmetician, academician, physician, adventitious, unpropitious, suspicious, brazier, glazier, profusion, allusion, opinion, civilian, disunion, collier, familiar.

Ambition, rotation, caution, negation, fashion, vision, relation, oration, emission, nation, passion, probation, erection, reckon, arrogation, organ, confession, ovation, lotion, perception, determination, deception, dissipation, exception, exhibition, perturbation, selection, silken, liken, rational, notional, mission, provisional, effusions, emissions, institutions, investigations, instigation, transactions, consideration, contortion, affection, rejection, dejection, emulation, inclination, recreation, direction, station, stations, reformation, reservation, demonstration, confiscation, exclusion, seclusion, construction, resolution, com-

prehension, preparation, assumption, operation, reduction.

RULE 2. Omit the dot vowels when not initial.

REMARK.—In words of infrequent occurrence it is often well to use the dot, and in many short words. Words of one syllable require vocalizing more carefully than words of two or more syllables; and, generally, the longer a word is, the more easily vowels may be spared. This remark applies to all the rules for omitting vowels.

RULE 3. Omit all vowels that do not readily join in the outline, except in short words of infrequent occurrence, or when initial.

EXERCISE TWENTY-FIRST.

Omit the dot vowels in the following words:—

Banishment, punishment, instrument, sentiment, compliment, dialect, intellect, pungency, currency, regency, decency, potency, fluency, orient.
Buffet, tablet, ticket, docket, sonnet, billet, garret, &c. *Congress, witness, fortress,* &c., *careless, homeless, needless, baseless,* &c. *Defensive, oppressive. When, whence, hence,* &c.

Insert the dot vowel in the following words:—

Every, edify, edible, etch, ebony, epsom, elf, &c. *Err, air,* &c. *Hair, fair, care,* &c.

Omit the disjoined vowels in the following words:—

Addition, emission, condition, furnish, garnish, tarnish, decision, recognition, composition.

MISCELLANEOUS.—*Carefulness, faithfulness, gracelessness, composure, consequence, composition, condensation, lamentable, constitutionality, concomitant, non-committal.*

A true gentleman is God's servant, the world's master, and his own man; his virtue is his business: his study his recreation; contentedness his rest, and happiness his reward. God is his father, and the Church his mother; the saints his brethren; all that need him his friends. He is necessitated to take the world in his way to heaven; but he walks through it as fast as he can.

RULE 4. Unaccented vowels in *long words* may be sometimes omitted, even when they could be joined in the writing.

This rule applies to most of the frequently occurring prefixes and affixes of derivative words, such as *com* and *con* with all their compounds, *decom, discom, discon,* &c., *circum, contra,* &c., with the terminations *ing, ed, es, ness, less,* &c.

Examples.

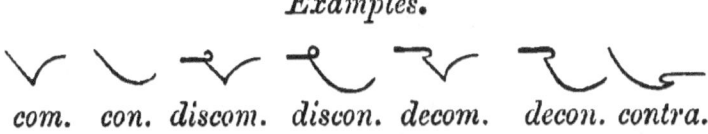

com.   con.   discom.   discon.   decom.   decon.   contra.

The Tachygrapher will notice that the use of the vowel is frequently an aid in the formation of the outline, and should be very careful not to omit vowels that are necessary on account of forming better angles.

EXERCISE TWENTY-SECOND.

Notwithstanding, nevertheless, remarkable, unconditional, disconnectedly, accommodating, unconstitutionality, comprehensive, apprehensive, persuasory, persuasive, persuade, disquiet, peculiarity, linguist, vanquish.

Passing, facing, racing, rising, hissing, guessing, being, beings, having, loving, living, moving, teaching, touching, canvassing, knowing, weighing, laughing, quaffing, commencing, convincing, composing, confessing, supposing, accordingly.

In-com-plete, in-con-stant, in-com-bustible, incompatible, incompetency, incomprehensible, inconceivable, inconclusive, incongruity, inconsiderable, inconsistent, inconvenience. *Uncommon, unconfined, uncommunicated, unconcerned, unconscious.* *Dis-com-pose, discommode, disconcert, discontent, discomposure.*

Disparity, principality, incomprehensibility, barbarity, dexterity, credulity, fragility, majority, locality, frugality, vulgarity, inseverity, servility, liberality, morality, immorality, cordiality, humility, temerity, minority, criminality, sensuality, inequality, recklessness, carelessly, wickedness, indebtedness, impressiveness.

THE OMISSION OF VOWELS IN SHORT WORDS OF FREQUENT OCCURRENCE.

115. It is better to write the vowels in words of one syllable in most cases; but there are a few brief words of so frequent occurrence that they become too familiar to need vocalization. The student may memorize the following, and write them as they are given on the top of page 14 of the Reading-Lessons.

Be, go, can, could, come, do, done, to, of, for, from, should, shall, is, so, some, though, they, that, them, then, there, may, many, on, any, not, unto, we, were, one, he, her, you, your, when, where.

REMARK.—Some persons may wish to increase this list for their own private writing; but it is very desirable that only recognized abbreviations of this kind should be introduced into general correspondence. The widest experience strengthens the conviction that it is safer to err by vocalizing too much than too little; yet the writer that wishes a fair degree of speed should make the most of the abbreviations given, and not fall into the loose habit of using the vowel at one time, and omitting it at another. This remark will apply also to the briefer forms given in subsequent chapters.

CHAPTER IX.

PHRASE-WRITING.

116. THE one distinguishing glory of our common chirography is its *continuity*. We may write a line without lifting the pen from the paper, if we omit to dot the *i*'s and to cross the *t*'s. This freedom of running one letter into another, and one word into another, adds greatly to the ease of writing, and mitigates, to some extent, the cumbersomeness of the letters employed. It would be desirable to imitate the common script in this respect. In Tachygraphy we are able to do so to better advantage than in any previous style of short-hand. The few disjoined vocals are omitted, so that the pen need not be raised to insert a vowel one-tenth as frequently as it is necessary to do so in the common writing to dot *i*'s and *j*'s or cross *t*'s.

It is allowable in Tachygraphy to join words together into phrases very frequently. Examples of such phrases will be found on the 13th page of the Reading-Lessons. The student should study this page thoroughly, before attending to the following principles.

The propriety of uniting words in writing, in any given case, is to be determined by the convenience, 1st, of the writer, 2d, of the reader.

1st, The convenience of the writer demands that the words unite either with a good angle, or without an angle. If the first word end in a vowel, or the second word begin with a vowel that cannot be joined, it is often necessary either to disjoin the words, or to omit the vowel.

The writer is not aided by making too long forms: long phrases detract from the speed of writing more than they add to it.

The convenience of the writer, then, demands, *a*, that the words joined shall make good combinations and facile forms; *b*, that the phrases shall be so brief and simple, that they shall not embarrass the writer.

2d, The convenience of the reader.

An observance of the above principles will aid the reader; but, besides these, it is essential to ease in reading *phrases* that no words be joined that are separated in speaking by a pause of any kind. It is not sufficient that the common marks of punctuation be observed: it is equally important to observe where a good reader pauses, and what words are united in sense. And here it will be observed that there are several degrees of closeness in the union of words. We have, —

First, a class called *adverbial phrases*, that seem to form in sense one word. Such are the following : —

In fine, in short, no doubt, in fact, in truth, to be sure, by chance, &c.

Second, The preposition and its object are closely united in sense.

Examples.

To them, of this, from that, for one, with me, through them, &c.

Third, The pronoun and the verb.

Examples.

I am, I have, you are, he is, they can, we may, who wish, &c.

Fourth, The same phrases in the interrogative form, *have I? are you?* &c.

So we might specify many other forms of speech which may form phrases properly. But such details would only embarrass the writer. If the words unite at all in sense, or are not positively separated in speech, they may be joined, in writing, into phrases of convenient length, so far as they join readily. If, on the contrary, they are the most closely united in sense, and do not join easily, or form long and cumbrous phrases, they should be disjoined in writing. The student must rely for a time upon the phrases given in the Reading-Lessons, and those indicated in the following exercise, and, so far as he forms phrases for himself, study simplicity and brevity, avoiding every long phrase or awkward combination.

EXERCISE TWENTY-THIRD.

(1.) *Of the, on the, to the, to a, of it, of this, of that, of me, to me, to know, to do, with this, with that, for this, for them, from it, from them, in this, in such, in fact, in fine, in short, in truth, on me, on any, in the, in no way.*

(2.) *I am, I shall, I do, I can, you are, you may, you could. He will, he should, he has. We know, we love, we learn. They should, they are, they ought. It is, it was, it may, it can, it has. The way, the time, the day, the present. There are, there may be.*

(3.) *Would you, would they, could we, can we, can they, shall we, could you, can be, cannot be.*

(4.) *It seems to be, ought to be, in the world, if there is. It would not be, with reference to, it is impossible, it is necessary, it is unnecessary. On account.*

(5.) *Let it be known, come unto me, give them their choice.*

My son, forget not my law, but let thine heart keep my commandments; for length of days, and long life, and peace shall they add to thee. Let not mercy and truth forsake thee; bind them about thy neck; write them upon the table of thine heart; so shalt thou find favor, and good understanding, in the sight of God and man.

Trust in the Lord with all thine heart, and lean not to thine own understanding. In all thy ways acknowledge him, and he shall direct thy paths.

NOTE.— See paragraph 92 of the Reading-Lessons, in the end of the book.

I shall be there to-day. We wish to see you. So far from that, one should choose some other road to happiness. They never know the cause of their calamities.

ABBREVIATED WORDS AND PHRASES.

117. REMARK.— We have given, in paragraphs 93 and 94 of the Reading-Lessons, a few abbreviated forms for some words and phrases, of frequent occurrence, whose fully-written forms are too long for note-taking. They should not be considered as forming any necessary part of the common style, as it can be written without them. Yet, if thoroughly mastered, they will add somewhat to the speed of writing for those who care to employ them.

KEY TO PARAGRAPH 93.— WORD-SIGNS.

And, as, has, have, this, what, had, would, which, will, been, ye, who.

NOTES.— *And* is written by a half-length ⌣ made heavy; *what, had,* and *would,* by halving the stem of their first letter. *Have, ye,* and *who* are written with the vowel-sign, omitting the consonant; *as, has,* and *this* employ the circle for *z* and *s*; *been* is written with the first letter only, and *which* and *will* by the last letter.

KEY TO PARAGRAPH 94, TO BE USED AS

WRITING-EXERCISE TWENTY-FOURTH.

As well as, as soon as, as we, has been, have been, you have, you've, we have, we've, I have, I've. They will be, you will be, we shall have been. This is, this is not to be, and they were, as they say, as some say, for instance, at first, at once, to be sure, to have been, and it is said, what would be, what had been, who would be, who are, ye are, at which, to which it is.

What is it? had it, had it not been, would it not be? This will be. Come unto me, all ye that labor and are heavy laden, and I will give you rest. Take my yoke upon you and learn of me, for I am meek and lowly in heart, and ye shall find rest unto your souls.

REMARK. — The last six pages of the Reading-Lessons will further illustrate the use of phrase-signs, both in their simple and more contracted forms. We add a Key to a part of pages 15 and 16, to serve as

WRITING-EXERCISE TWENTY-FIFTH.

A DISTINCTION. — *A Roman ecclesiastic, in reply to whatever question might be proposed, began by saying, " Distinguo," — I make a distinction. A cardinal, having invited him to dine, proposed to derive some amusement for the company from the well-known peculiarity of his guest; and, saying to him that he had an important question to propose, he asked, " Is it, in any circumstances, lawful to baptize in soup?" — " I make a distinction," said the priest : " if you ask, Is it lawful to baptize in soup in general, I say, No; but if you ask, Is it lawful to baptize in your Excellency's soup, I say, Yes; for there is really no difference between it and water."*

IMPEDIMENTS TO REFORM. — *When George Stephenson was presenting the claims for the first locomotive to the British Parliament, he was sneered at by many members. Said one of them, " Well, Mr. Stephenson, see how absurd your idea is! Suppose it were possible for you to run your carriage thirty miles an hour, on straight rails, so that it could not get off,—what if a cow got on the track, and you could not turn out for her?"—" Well, my lords," said Stephenson, " it would be* bad for the cow."

CHAPTER X.

THE VARIABLE LETTERS. — EQUIVOCAL WORD-FORMS.

118. One element in the simplicity of Tachygraphy consists in avoiding, so far as possible, equivocal forms for words. They cannot, however, be wholly avoided. A difference of outline is rendered possible if the word contains any letter that can be written in more than one way ; and, if a word contains two or more variable letters, the forms it is capable of assuming increase in geometrical ratio. Thus, in Phonography, a word containing the letters *s, t, r, d* (e. g., *stride, storied, Saturday,* &c.), may assume twenty different forms, since two of these letters have more than one form, and all may be combined with others in various ways.

This indefiniteness is reduced in Tachygraphy to the narrowest limits by relying upon fixed principles in the use of equivocal letters, so that, though several forms might be possible, the proper form will generally be obvious at once.

VARIABLE LETTERS.

119. The variable letters are ⌠ ⌡ and ╱, which

are written either upward or downward; and ⌐ and ⌐, which are reversed into ⌐ and ⌐.

When ⌐ ⌐ and ⌐ are written upward, they are called *Ma, La,* and *Ra;* when written downward, they are called *Em, El,* and *Ar.*

Whether the upward or downward forms of these letters should be used, is a question to be determined wholly by convenience; but this *convenience* is determined by the following principles:—

EM, EL, AR, MA, LA, AND RA.

120. It is desirable that that form should be used, that,

1. Joins most readily, and forms the most graceful and facile word-form; and that,

2. Best corrects the tendency of the other letters to run too far above or too far below the line of writing.

1. These letters connect, *a.* with vocal, *b.* with consonantal letters.

a. (1.) After ⌐ ⌐ ⌐ ⌐ and ⌐ *Ma* is used. *Em* always follows ⌐.

Ma is used before ⌐ ⌐ ⌐ and ⌐. With other vocals, *Em* and *Ma* are equally convenient.

(2.) After - and - *El* is used; and after ⌐ *La.* *La* is also used before ⌐ ⌐ ⌐ ⌐ and ⌐; and *El* before ⌐ ⌐ and ⌐. With other vocals, *El* and *La* are equally convenient.

(3.) *Ra* is used before ⌐ ⌐ ⌐ ⌐ ⌐, and after ⌐ ⌐ ⌐ ⌐ ⌐ and ⌐. *Ar*, only, follows ⌐ - and - . In other cases, *Ar* and *Ra* are equally convenient.

When *r* commences a word, *Ra* is almost always used.

b. When the direction of these letters is determined by their union with other consonant letters, they are written upward both before and after all the down strokes, and before the hooked letters *Wa, Ya, Ha, Cha,* and *Ja.* With the horizontals, that direction should generally be preferred that makes the acutest angle. Thus we use *Ar* after *De, Te, Ja,* and *Cha,* and *Ra* after *Ze* and *Es.* We write *Ra-Te,* however, when *R* is initial, although *Ar-Te* would make an acuter angle.

SPECIAL CASES.

121. (1.) When *r*, not initial, is followed by *d* or *t*, in such words as *card, recurred, recorded, discord,* &c., the *Ar* makes more facile and compact forms than *Ra.* It will be often safe to use the *Ar* in this way even in words like *regard* and *record,* where the vowel must be omitted.

(2.) When *rd* or *rt* follows ╱ or ╱ , in such words as *word, ward, heard,* &c., the *Ar* is always convenient.

(3.) In words like *hurl, whirl,* &c., it will be seen that *Ha-Ra-El* is better than *Ha-Ar-La.* So, in *world,* we write *Wa-Ra-El-De.*

ITH AND THE, THA AND GA.

122. The inversion of the alphabetic letters *Ith* and *The* adds very much to the beauty of outline and facileness of form of the class of words containing these sounds. They occur less frequently than the variable letters mentioned above, and their use is determined by the same principles of combination as those that decide whether *El, Em,* and *Ar,* or *Ma, La* and *Ra,* are prefer-

able. They are the following, and are capable of universal application, — to vocals as well as consonantals, — so far as any letter may be varied to produce better angles.

PRINCIPLES DETERMINING THE USE OF VARIABLE LETTERS.

123. The principles of joining, given in paragraphs 73 to 83, are the basis of the following applications: —

We have (*a.*) Straight lines joined with straight lines. (*b.*) Straight lines joined with curves. (*c.*) Curves joined with curves.

(*a.*) RIGHT LINES JOINED.

(1.) Straight lines that unite without an angle are most convenient. Hence *Ra* is struck upward after *Ra*, *Wa*, *Ha*, and *Wha*, when no other principle interferes. As we have seen in paragraph 121, this principle is overcome by another equally important in cases where — or — follows *R*; namely, —

(2.) *Acute* angles are to be preferred to obtuse angles. Now, *Ha-Ar-Te* gives us two acute angles, and *Ha-Ra-Te* only one angle, *but an obtuse one;* and, in this case, we prefer the two acute angles to the one obtuse angle. In the words *hurt* and *heard*, this principle applies; but, in the word *hurried*, we may relieve the obtuse angle by inserting the last vowel, and so use *Ra* instead of *Ar*.

REMARK. — The use of a vowel may often relieve a bad angle, even in cases where there are no variable letters, except the vocals. This is seen in such words as *tick*, *back*, *rid*, *width*, *hid*, *whit*, &c.; and it is a great error to omit the vowel in such words, for it not only leaves the word indefinite, but produces a form more inconvenient for the writer than the fully vocalized forms.

(*b.*) RIGHT LINES JOINED TO CURVES.

(1.) Here we have only acute angles, if any at all, since the obtuse angles are rounded off, and disappear. And here an acute angle is preferred, in some cases, to those forms that exclude the angle. Notice the use of the vocal in the words *form* and *dollar*, in Exercises Twelfth and Thirteenth, and the use of *Ef-Ra-Ma*, instead of *Ef-Ar-Ma*, in *firm, firmly*. *De-El* and *Te-El* is preferred to *De-La* and *Te-La;* but there is no difficulty in writing *De-Ith*.

(2.) As the dash-vocals must always make angles when joined, they are more frequently omitted with the *curves* than with the *right lines*.

(*c.*) CURVES JOINED WITH CURVES.

These are distinguished into (1.) facing curves, (2.) opposing curves.

(1.) When curves are of such directions that they would make, if straight, an obtuse angle, they should be *facing* if possible. We prefer, for instance, *Es-Ith* to *Es-Tha*.

And facing curves are better also with right or acute angles, for then they unite into half-circles or ellipses. Facing curves are always convenient.

(2.) Opposing curves are convenient when in the same direction, for they may unite without angles, as in the case of *Es-En*.

Opposing curves whose lines of direction would form right or acute angles are tolerable; but opposing curves whose lines of direction would form obtuse angles are to be avoided if possible.

By reversing the direction of *Em* and *El*, we change the direction in which the curve faces. *La-En* are curves facing in the same direction. *El-En* are opposing curves. So in any case where the sounds of *l* or *m*, *th* or *a*, occur, they may be changed so as to form facing curves, if desired. So the use of variable characters, which seems to be, from one point of view, a *necessity*, and tolerable only as necessary, becomes one of the greatest means of securing grace and beauty of outline.

REMARK. — We give for the first part of Writing-Exercise Twenty-sixth a Key to Reading-Lessons Twelfth and Thirteenth. The student should first write the exercise without referring to the reading-lesson, and then compare his exercise with the printed forms, and correct his errors.

EXERCISE TWENTY-SIXTH.
(See page 10 of the Reading-Lessons.)

73. *Melancholy, mellifluous, multiplication, multitude, merit, mellow, meritorious, territory, tariff, military.*

74. *Remark, remove, re-arrange, raiment, relative, learn, large, lark, look, lower, leer, lyric, lost.*

75. *Toll, tall, soul, Saul, bowl, ball, hole, hall, cold.*

76. *Aim, name, fame, blame, am, ham, dam, lamb, dame, lame, deem, seem, stream, ream, scream, memory, remember, freedom, kingdom, random, amendment, rarefy, mirror, murmur, miller, dollar, horror, redeemer, reclaimer, clamor, brigadier.*

77. When Freedom from her mountain height
Unfurled her standard to the air,
She tore the azure robe of night,
And set the stars of glory there.

She mingled with its gorgeous dyes
The milky baldrick of the skies,
And striped its pure celestial white
With streakings of the morning light

78. *Form, formal, firm, firmly, reform, deform, inform, misform, familiar, familiarity, dissimilarity, humility.*

79. *Letter, litter, literal, lateral, latterly, alter, leader, elder, easel, easily, vassal, tassel, seldom, soldier, Philadelphia.*

80. *Alienate, million, rebellion, companion, failure.*

81. *Epicure, occupy, manual, residue, purify, curious, endure, nature, refuse, union, unite, re-unite, ubiquity, reward, rewarder, rehearse, rejoin, moonlight, twilight, homeward, lampblack, journal, heirloom.*

Disciplinarian, contradictory, metropolitan, arithmetical, mathematical.

Improve, ambition, I'm, aim, motive, mutter, lay, land, longitude, lewd, loud, lee, linnet, lowered, fold, foul, full.

Ray, radical, roll, ran, irrelevant, architecture, arrival, Ireland, arouse, various, carrier, ream, hymn, raise, risk.

Wear, fair, rare, hair, tory, weary, year, your, chair, germ, jeer, cherry, tarry, attire, tare, dare, infidelity, telegraphy.

Athens, writhe, soothe, tooth, wisheth, meaneth, soweth, feareth, theft, theist, atheist, isothermal, æsthetic.

The way, the heart, the portion, the first, the best, the easiest, the right, the glory, the blessing.

CHAPTER XI.

CONCLUDING INSTRUCTIONS.

124. HAVING explained and illustrated all the principles that enter into this style of the art, it only remains for us to add a few miscellaneous instructions, and further directions for practice.

The student has learned to omit all silent letters, and to employ the proper phonic signs for each sound; but some cases of difficulty may still occur. We notice a few special cases.

WHEN THE SAME CONSONANT IS REPEATED.

a. In this case, in such words as *opportunity, attend, annual,* &c., it is customary to write only one *p*, one *t*, and one *n*. And so almost universally only one consonant is written in Tachygraphy, when the letter is repeated in the common orthography.

There are, however, a few cases where both letters are clearly sounded. In such cases both should be written, as in the words *wholly, fully, misstate, unnecessary, unnatural.*

In words commencing with the prefixes *il* and *im*, as *illegal, immoral,* the *l* and *m* are sounded twice, and may be written twice in Tachygraphy; but it is not necessary to legibility.

b. The letter *n* has several varieties of sound. Before the sound of *g hard*, it approximates very nearly to the sound of *Ing*, and is written with this letter. Examples, — *language, longer.*

Before *k* and *c* it has a lighter nasal sound, which is also written by *Ing;* though this letter does not express the sound very accurately. Examples, — *bank, succinct.* The true sound of *Ing* is heard when the *g* blends with the *n* and is lost in it, as in *sing, song.*

REMARK. — It will be noticed that the letters *ng* are pronounced in three ways, as in the words *sing, singe, longer;* written with *Ing, En-Ja,* and *En-Ga.*

c. The letter *c* has four different sounds, as in the words *come, ace, occan,* and *suffice,* — the sounds of *Ka, E's, Ish,* and *Ze.*

d. The letter *x,* which is generally sounded liks *ks,* has sometimes the sound of *Gz,* — *extra, exalt.*

PUNCTUATION.

125. All the marks of punctuation may be used in Tachygraphy as they are used in the common writing, except the dash, which should commence with a waved line to distinguish it from the letter *Te.*

The *diæresis* and *apostrophe* are not used; and the *hyphen* is made as in the German, thus ".

MANUAL DRILL.

126. If the student has attended faithfully to the preceding principles, he will know how to write correctly nearly every word in the language. But he should not be disappointed to find that his attention to principles has interfered with his practice, and left him with a more theoretical than practical knowledge of RAPID WRITING. He should now review the whole ground, and endeavor to gain the skill in manipulation necessary to rapidity of writing. To aid him in this, we offer the following directions : —

a. Train the fingers, if necessary, by such exercises as are given by teachers of *Penmanship.* Some practice in long-hand writing is necessary to give freedom of motion.

It is absolutely necessary that the writer feel perfectly free to use his pen as he chooses. He must unite a degree of *carelessness* with his *carefulness,* to secure any grace, and freedom of form. To secure this result, let him *scribble fifteen minutes* before every writing-exercise, not loosely, but methodically, using a large variety of exercises.

b. Manual Drill, when perfected on the old exercises, should be turned to advantage in Tachygraphy, as follows : —

(1.) Drill on the alphabet as directed in Chapter IV.

(2.) Drill on the combinations of the vocals with the consonantals.

(3.) Join the consonants into the most natural angles, and learn to make two letters without the slightest pause between them.

REMARK. — This will afford scope for much practice. The teacher should draw up tables of such combinations as he may deem most important, and give a dozen or more examples with each lesson.

(4.) Join the consonants also that unite without an angle, and practise on them until both strokes can be struck as though they were but one.

REMARK. — It may be well here to select phrases containing such joinings, and let the pupil drill on a number of phrases until he can write them at the rate of a hundred words a minute. Most persons will do this readily. We add a few phrases, making about a hundred words, which will serve as a specimen of this kind of practice.

EXERCISE TWENTY-SEVENTH.

To this day, from this time, from that day, at this time, in some way, it is not, he should do, to do so, ought to do, it ought to be. They will be (Tha-La-Be). *This is not to be, we shall have been, may there be, let there be.*

Come forward, from them, from them that, from their own, there shall be, come unto me, give them their own, we wish for it, though they were not, try to do so, is it so soon? he cannot do less, we wish to do so, you will be there, he was too soon, to meet, his friends.

REMARK. — Some of these phrases are longer than they should generally be made. They are given as an exercise in manual drill, rather than as models for imitation. If the student finds some difficulty at first in getting through the longer forms, he will find a patient mastery of the difficulty conducive to speed in less difficult forms.

(5.) Practice on word-forms, whenever there is any difficulty in forming them, until the hand can trace them readily.

(6.) All practice, after the elements are mastered, is promoted by writing from dictation. The reader should read easy words and sentences just fast enough to incite the writer to his highest speed, without burdening his memory. To make reading profitable, it should be natural. In reading sentences, regard should be had to the sense. If the reader attempts to accommodate the writer by pausing after every word, no phrases can be formed, and all the value of the reading will be lost.

REMARK. — The teacher should, if possible, spend some time in dictating for his class to write. He should, at least, show how this work can be done to the best advantage. Where students are without a teacher, it will save time if several can meet for practice, either employing a dictator to read for all, or taking turns at dictation. It will frequently be well to have each word or phrase repeated three times. This will enable the reader to accommodate writers of different degrees of ability. Some will be able to keep pace with him, others to write the word twice, and still others only once out of the three times the word or phrase is uttered by the reader. The *words* can be repeated only where they stand isolated. In reading sentences, the dictator should read clauses containing five to ten words, and then repeat the clause.

Those who have neither teacher nor associates in the study of the art should interest some friend in reading for them.

(7.) The student who observes these directions, and practises the preceding Writing-Exercises until he can write them correctly and readily, will have a fair command of the style. If he wishes to acquire greater speed, he should extend his practice, writing from dictation (no other practice will answer in place of this) from other books; commencing with those of more simple language, and going on into any field of literature that he may care to cultivate. Or he may take notes of lectures and sermons. Some have reported whole courses of lectures successfully by the use of the principles taught in the Compendium, in which were introduced fewer brief forms than are given in this work. Rest assured that a speed of eighty or ninety words a minute can be attained in this style sooner, and retained longer, than in any other style whatsoever. Speed in any style can only come through perfect familiarity with the forms used.

FACILITY IN READING.

127. Skill in reading, as in writing, can come only through practice. You have in this system word-forms that are entirely distinctive. The same form rarely, if ever, stands for more than one word. Hence the reader need not rely upon the context, but may always be *certain* at once of the true reading. But, as the letters become somewhat obscured in rapid writing, he must

gain a familiarity with the word-forms. We do this in the common print. We seldom stop to note the letters of a word, but take in its general form, as we know the face of a friend without noting the individual peculiarity of his features.

CONCLUSION.

128. While we have treated in the preceding pages, as fully as possible, of all the elements of the art, we know that the student will find a world of beauty to which we have only pointed out the way.

The practice of the art will be an ever-increasing pleasure. Use the time saved by your skill in writing in acquiring useful knowledge and in blessing your fellow-men.

APPENDIX

TO THE ELEMENTS OF TACHYGRAPHY.

[The following specifications were omitted from the first two editions of the work.]

THE POSITION OF OUTLINES.

129. The outline of a word is its form as it stands on the written page. It is a question often, with the young writer, as to the position which this outline shall assume to the line of writing. The rule is very simple. If the word contains only one consonant stroke, that is written so as to rest on the line of writing: that is, if horizontal, it will be written near the line; if perpendicular, or inclined downward, it will *end* on the line; if inclined and struck upward, it will commence on the line, and thus rest on it. Note that the consonant stroke rests on the line, and the vowel falls below, or wherever its proper direction brings it.

130. If the word contain two or more consonant strokes, the outline rests upon the first perpendicular or inclined stroke, if it contain such a stroke; if all the letters are horizontal, they are written near the line. So we have the following general rule: *The first perpendicular or inclined consonant stroke rests upon the line of writing.*

131. In cases where several horizontal strokes precede the inclined or perpendicular one upon which the outline rests, the writer needs to consider whether to commence on the line, or above it. If the stroke upon which the outline rests is written downward, he will commence the word the length of one letter above the line; if the ruling stroke is upward, he will commence on the line.

132. All strokes after the ruling stroke follow their proper direction, according to the rules given previously. (See especially Chapter X.)

133. Where unruled paper is used, the same principle prevails. The words are always arranged with reference to a line, although no line appear.

The following examples illustrate the above remarks. But the student should notice the position of outlines in other examples scattered throughout the work, and in the Reading-Lessons.

Examples.

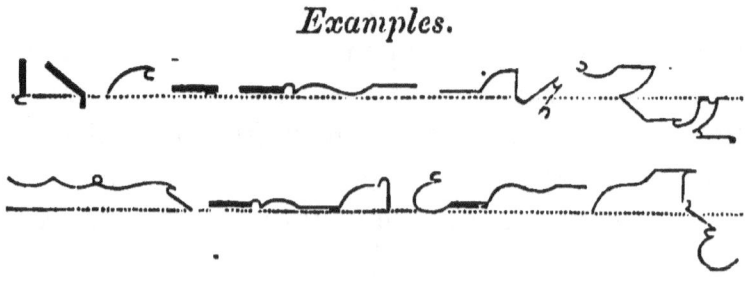

THE NEW SIGN FOR WHA.

134. We introduce with this edition (the third) a new sign for *Wha*, and have endeavored to make the necessary changes throughout the volume, where it could conveniently be done.

135. *a.* The old form was made by enlarging the hook of the *Ha*, and making it heavy. This produced a character too gross for rapid writing, while at the same time the hook on the right of the up-stroke was inconvenient in phrases.

b. The new letter is made by merely thickening the hook for the Wa; thus:

REMARK. — This gives us nearly the same form that is used in the old Phonography. Mr. Pitman made a hook on the left of the Ra, to imply *W* before *R*, and thickened this hook for *wh*.

136. The value of the new form will be appreciated in such words as *where, why, what, any-where, no-where;* and such phrases as *on-what-account, to-what, with-what,* &c., as given below: —

REMARK. — We can assure our friends that we have no wish to prosecute experiments in new forms, as the inventor of Phonography has done for so many years. The success of the art can be secured only through uniformity, and uniformity can be preserved only by adherence to established forms. The era of experiments has passed: let it not be revived. The time of a whole generation, devoted to it by the Phonographers, has developed the resources of the art in many directions. This work was doubtless necessary, but it has borne fruit in wide-spread and hopeless dissensions among the writers of the old Phonography. We hope, through the favor of God, to be spared from a repetition of a work already overdone, and trust that no innovator will ever mar this style by crude attempts at improvement.

No letter of the alphabet has been changed since the publication of the system in 1864. The above is our only change. We have, however, made some changes in the briefer styles, in preparing them for the press, which we trust will render these styles even more complete and rapid than they have been heretofore written, as taught through the manuscripts.

A reporting style *must* change from time to time, to meet new exigencies. Words and phrases are of frequent occurrence at one time that fall into comparative disuse at another. We do not hope for any absolute standard in the briefest forms. But the style explained in the preceding pages need not change, except as the language upon which it rests changes, slowly, and, to most persons, imperceptibly. We ask all our friends to unite in one purpose to maintain, not uniformity in the science as expressed in books merely, but — what is more difficult of achievement — uniformity of word-forms throughout the brotherhood of those who cultivate the art.

THE VOWEL U. — HOW WRITTEN.

137. There is a degree of indefiniteness in the pronunciation of this vowel; some persons inclining more to the use of -, and others to the use of ∧. We do not assume to settle questions of orthoepy. We distinguish such words as *do* and *dew*, *coo* and *cue*, *who* and *hew*, *rood* and *rude*, &c., by employing the simple vowel - in the former word of these couplets, and the ∧ in the latter.

138. There are, however, very many cases of longer words, where either - or ∧ may be used according to convenience, without any effort to secure precision of pronunciation. We use, for instance, the - in the words *communion*, *communicate*, *renewal*, *allusion*,

THE VOWEL U. — HOW WRITTEN.

delusion, &c., although a strict pronunciation would demand ∧ ; and generally, where – is more easily written than ∧, it may be used. The shorter sign is generally to be preferred in words of more than one syllable, when it can be easily joined in the outline.

139. The letters ⌐ and ⌐ join more easily with –; and yet the ∧ must be used in such words as *lieu, lewd, lure, nude*. It should be especially noticed, however, the ∧ is never used with ⌐, except in the word *yew*. *Union*, and all words commencing with long *u* before which the sound ⌐ occurs, are written as though spelled *younion, youniti*, &c.

140. This sound of *u* is frequent in the midst of words, as also in the termination *-ure*.

Examples.

occupy   reputation   manumit   natural

REMARK 1. — The termination *-ure* is misunderstood by some persons. Wishing to avoid the vulgar pronunciation **nachur, cap-chur**, &c., they avoid also the *y*, and write *na-ture, cap-ture*. This is an error. The true sounds are *nāt-yur, capt-yur*. The *-yur* in these examples is to be pronounced so short as to leave the sound of *u* nearly silent.

There are some words, however, in which this termination is long, as, for example, *literature, caricature*. These words have been pronounced by good authorities without the *y*-sound, thus: *lit-er-a-tūre, car-i-ca-tūre;* but I prefer to write them with the ⌐, in analogy with *nāt-ure* and words of this class, though the *-ure* may be pronounced longer than in the other cases mentioned.

REMARK 2. — The affected pronunciation of *dyooty* for *duty* is a vulgarism that will be avoided by all. The letter *u* never has the sound of *yoo* in the midst of a syllable after a consonant. Hence the words *duty, tune,* and all words of this kind, are written with the ᴧ or - simply.

WRITING-EXERCISE TWENTY-EIGHTH.

Coo, cue, rood, rude, mood, mewed, sewed, crude, brood, brewed, food, viewed, clew, flew, slew, pew, crew, screw, drew, shrew, stew, jew, blew, blue, suit, soot, cube, tube. Lieu, lure, nude, yew. Renewal, allusion, effusion, illusion, delusion, confusion. Union, unite, unify. Communion, communicate, intercommunication. Duty, duteous, dutiful, beautiful, tune.

Reputation, occupy, secular, estuary, spiritual, speculation, manumission, manufacture, nature, natural, structure, literature, temperature, caricature, horticulture, agriculture, agricultural. Regularly, regulation, graduation, congratulation.

ABBREVIATED FORMS FOR -NESS, -LESS, AND DIS-.

141. *a.* According to the principle stated in sec. 113 (page 78), the circle may be used for *s* in the terminations *-less, -ness, -lessness, -lessly.*

Examples.—*Goodness, witness, carelessness, carelessly.*

b. The circle may also be used in such words as *access, success,* and *accession, succession,* as in the examples below.

142. In some cases, where the first form of a word ends with the circle, and another *s* or *es* is added, as in the word *witnesses,* it is inconvenient to add the letter ⌒. In such cases, the circle may be enlarged to twice its usual size to indicate the added *s.*

ABBREVIATED FORMS FOR -NESS, -LESS, ETC.

Examples.

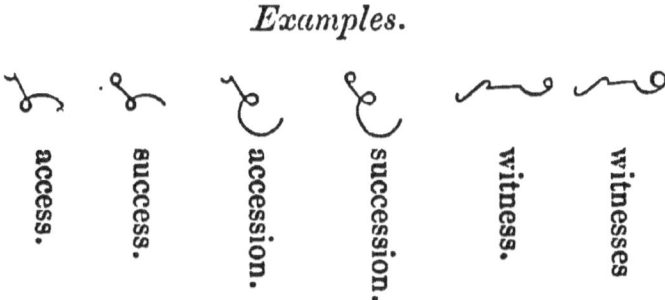

access. success. accession. succession. witness. witnesses

143. In analogy with the use of the circle in *discom-* and *discon-* (as given on page 83), the circle may also be used in the prefix *dis-* in such words as *discuss, distance,* and wherever it is more convenient than the full form; so also in the prefix *mis-* in *misfortune, misconceive,* &c.

144. *a.* The circle may also be used in the words *person, parson, Johnson,* and all similar words where the termination *-son* follows *r* or *n* without an intervening vowel; but *comparison, Tennyson,* and words having a vowel before this termination, are written with the ⌒.

b. When to a word ending with the circle the termination *-ing* is added, the circle is retained. The circle is written, in accordance with this rule, in the following words; *tax taxing, force forcing, nursing, coalescing, caressing, witnessing,* and many others.

REMARK. — These brief forms are given as an aid to those persons who wish to gain a high rate of speed in the COMMON STYLE. Those who design to pass on at once to the NOTE-TAKER'S STYLE will learn the use of the circle in its more general application.

READING LESSONS.

Reading Lessons.

Lesson First.

(shorthand characters)

Lesson Second.

(shorthand characters)

Lesson Third.

13. [shorthand]
14. [shorthand]
15. [shorthand]
16. [shorthand]
17. [shorthand]
18. [shorthand]
19. [shorthand]

Lesson Fourth.

20. [shorthand]
21. [shorthand]
22. [shorthand]
23. [shorthand]
24. [shorthand]
25. [shorthand]
26. [shorthand]
27. [shorthand]

Lesson Fifth.

28. [shorthand]
29. [shorthand]
30. [shorthand]
31. [shorthand]
32. [shorthand]
33. [shorthand] but [shorthand]
34. [shorthand]
35. [shorthand]
36. [shorthand] "!" [shorthand] "1, 1, 1, [shorthand]; [shorthand]."

Lesson Sixth.

37. [shorthand]
38. [shorthand]
39. [shorthand]
40. [shorthand]
41. [shorthand]

St. John's Gospel. Chap. 1.

42. [shorthand] . 2. [shorthand] . 3. [shorthand] . 4. [shorthand] . 5. [shorthand] . 6. [shorthand] . 7. [shorthand] . 8. [shorthand]

Lesson Seventh.

43.
44.
45.
46.
47.
48.
49.

Lesson Eighth.

50.
51.
52.
53.

Lesson Ninth.

54. [shorthand]

55. [shorthand]

56. [shorthand]

The Lord's Prayer.

57. [shorthand] VI. 9–13.

LESSON TENTH.

58. [shorthand characters]

59. [shorthand characters]

60. [shorthand characters] 61. [shorthand characters]

62. [shorthand characters]

63. [shorthand characters] 64. [shorthand characters]

65. [shorthand characters] 66. [shorthand characters]

67. [shorthand characters] 68. [shorthand characters]

69. [shorthand characters]

LESSON ELEVENTH.

70.

71.

The Past and Present. — *Mackay.*

72.

Lesson Twelfth.

73.

74.

75.

76.

Our Country's Flag.—Drake.

77.

LESSON THIRTEENTH.

78.

79.

80.

81.

LABOR. — Osgood.

82.

LESSON FOURTEENTH.

83.

84.

Ambition. — Byron.

85.

Words Joined in Phrases.

86.

87.

88.

89.

Be Equal to the Crisis.

90.

Vowels Omitted.

91.

92.

93. Word Signs.

94.

A Distinction.

Impediments to Reform.

The Golden Age.

The Flower. — Tennyson.

THE ELEMENTS OF TACHYGRAPHY.

WE give below a few extracts from notices of the Elements of Tachygraphy. The Third Edition of this work, containing an Appendix and newly engraved Reading Lessons, is now ready, and may be obtained of the Publishers, Otis Clapp & Son, 3 Beacon St., Boston; D. Kimball, P. O. Box 398, Chicago; and at the office of the Rapid Writer, Andover, Mass.

NOTICES OF THE PRESS.

From the Springfield Republican, Mass.

Otis Clapp, No. 3 Beacon Street, Boston, the old-time publisher of phonographic works, has just issued a neat little text-book, entitled the *Elements of Tachygraphy*. The system of shorthand developed in this work is the result of years of careful and critical investigation. The author was at one time an enthusiastic follower of Isaac Pitman, of England, who, a little over thirty years ago, reduced the arbitrary stenographies of former ages to a basis approaching scientific accuracy. . . . Even with its pretensions to simplicity, phonography was found altogether too complex in its arrangements. First, the signs employed, though universally acknowledged as a correct basis, were married to sounds utterly unfitted for them. Instead of representing those sounds that occur most frequently by horizontal strokes, thus conducing to lineality of writing, a very important requisite of ease and rapidity, perpendicular characters were supplied, which, when words were fully written, produced forms the most awkward and unmanageable. To obviate this, numerous devices of contraction were resorted to, which at once destroyed that simplicity so essential to a system of writing that aspires to common use. In the next place, vowel signs were disconnected in the writing, much to the detriment of speed, or were they omitted as cumbersome, ambiguity inevitably resulted. These were the radical imperfections of Pitman's Phonography thirty years ago; and, although its author has made numerous modifications and imaginary improvements since, they still continue to be the chief objections. This is also the case with Graham and Munson, and several other inventors of systems in this country, who, however well they have administered to the wants of a few professional reporters, have entirely ignored that great class of business, professional, and literary men, chiefly to be benefited by such an invention. Tachygraphy, however, avoiding these stumbling-blocks of its predecessors, has at last developed into that ideal writing which has filled the brains of phoneticians for these many years. At once the very embodiment of grace and beauty, its simplicity commends it to all, while the results already obtained in its practical use are extremely satisfactory. The book before us is devoted to the simplest style of the art, which it treats in a thorough and comprehensive manner. It offers a system of writing that may be readily written with three times the speed and one-fifth the labor of our common longhand, and which is more easily mastered than that. With suitable instruction it is within the comprehension of the merest child, while mature persons, though doubtless more secure of satisfactory results with the help of a competent teacher, can hardly fail to find it a complete guide.

From the Congregationalist and Recorder, Boston.

The art of saving time and trouble is a great art. And of all weariness, that of much writing — to many, at least — most needs alleviation, if possible. Shorthand, in various forms, has been invented and taught, without coming into general use. Of late years the system called Tachygraphy (or rapid writing) has been invented, and is believed, by those who have made themselves acquainted with it, to be destined to supersede every other system of condensed writing in meeting the wants of the world.

From the Boston Journal.

Mr. Otis Clapp, No. 3 Beacon Street, has just published *The Elements of Tachygraphy*, a full and compendious text-book upon the new and popular system of shorthand originated by Mr. D. P. Lindsley, formerly of this city. The system has been in use for several years, and its practical utility has been demonstrated beyond cavil by scores of writers. The principles, which are as simple as the multiplication table, are readily comprehended by the youngest learner, and can be mastered by any one in a very short time, and without a teacher. The system is especially adapted to the wants of students and literary men, in a great degree superseding the use of longhand, and it forms the basis of a briefer system for verbatim reporters.

From the Citizen and Round Table, New York.

Mr. David Philip Lindsley has prepared a little work, entitled *The Elements of Tachygraphy*, in which he explains an improved system of shorthand writing. *From a thorough examination of this system, we have no doubt that it will entirely supersede phonography.* It is vastly more simple, can be mastered in a comparatively short time, and can be written certainly as fast, if not faster, than the system of Pitman. Mr. Lindsley inspires one with confidence in the excellence of the art which he has invented, by the remarkable clearness and brevity of his explanations. His book needs only to become known, in order to ensure the adoption of Tachygraphy in place of the wearisome and difficult art of Phonography.

From the Christian Standard, Alliance, Ohio.

We once tried to master Phonography, but found it so intricate and perplexing that we could not afford to bestow enough time and attention to succeed But Mr. Lindsley has, as Horace Mann said, "phonographied Phonography," and it looks like an attainable art. Avoiding the contractions and word signs of Phonography, he teaches the student, as soon as the alphabet is mastered, to proceed at once to use the system. We do not pretend to be much of a judge, but a perusal of this book impresses us very favorably as to the practicability and value of Tachygraphy.

From the Presbyterian Banner, Pittsburg, Pa.

Tachygraphy is the classical title of a manual of 126 pages, upon shorthand writing, by D. P. Lindsley, published by Otis Clapp, Boston. It is the result of twelve years of study and practice, and it is claimed for this system that it is written in one fourth the time and with one tenth the labor of ordinary writing; is perfectly legible, and for use in the pulpit and lecture-room is plainer than longhand writing, and can be learned more readily than common writing. These considerations are sufficient to commend this system to all literary men.

From the Northwestern Christian Advocate, Chicago.

This excellent paper, after a long and favorable notice of the art, and its new text-book, makes the following *points* in reply to a correspondent who favors Graham's Phonography:—

"He (the critic) has simply compared Lindsley's most elementary style with the various (contracted) styles of other phonographies. As to 'corresponding styles,' we believe that there are none at all comparable with that in Tachygraphy. We indorse this because of its use to the masses. It is learned twice or thrice as soon as the same style in the old Phonography. In the reporting style, Tachygraphy is not inferior."

From the Meriden Daily Recorder.

Our opinion of the system of shorthand explained in this book has been given several times before, and a repetition of it now is unnecessary. Let it suffice for us to say that our conviction of the vast superiority of Tachygraphy over all other systems of brief writing is stronger than ever. Its superiority is acknowledged by all competent judges. Taken as a whole, it is certainly the most perfect shorthand text-book ever published. We heartily indorse the most flattering testimonials in its favor. The work is adapted to self-instruction, but this art, like all others, can be best acquired with the assistance of a living teacher.

From the Methodist, New York.

We commend this essay to learners.

From the Western Christian Advocate, Cin., Ohio.

Those who wish to become shorthandists will find Mr. Lindsley's manual just the thing.

From the East Boston Advocate.

After some examination of this and other systems of shorthand writing, we have unhesitatingly given this the preference over all others as being the most easily acquired, the simplest to write, and most practicable.

From the Atlantic Monthly, February, 1870.

We have a real pleasure in speaking of this system of shorthand. Its principles are so clear and simple that they can be understood with an hour's study. . . . Until a writing machine is invented, Mr. Lindsley's system must seem the greatest possible benefaction. Phonography is a science to which months of study must be given, and in the acquirement of which the memory is burdened with a multitude of arbitrary and variable signs; while in Tachygraphy the letters are almost invariable, and as easily memorized as the ordinary Roman characters; a single impulse of the hand forms each letter; there are as few detached marks as in the ordinary Chirography, and the writing is fluent and easy. . . . We feel certain that to editors, clergymen, and the whole vast and increasing body of literary men, it must prove a great advantage; and we commend it to the attention of teachers as a system which might very well be taught in schools.

From the Gazette and Courier, Northampton, Mass.

We cannot go into a critical examination of the merits of this system. We only wish that all who are groaning under the burdens of our common longhand, who are vexed by the irregularities of our cumbrous orthography, would send for and examine this little book.

We say nothing of the comparative merits of Phonography. After a ten years' use of that tedious method, an experience of three years with this later system has made us, perhaps, in some measure qualified to speak in its praise; and to say that there are good reasons for the one becoming, as it fast is, an extinct thing, and for the other steadily coming into general use.

From the Churchman, Hartford, Conn.

THE ELEMENTS OF TACHYGRAPHY, ETC. — If any person were to say that there are contained in this unpretending volume the elements of one of the greatest intellectual improvements of modern times, his assertion would seem to be extravagant. Yet those who have become familiar with the system of rapid writing, of which Mr. Lindsley is the inventor, know that the assertion is true to the letter.

Every one who is much engaged in literary composition is painfully conscious that the mechanical labor needed in putting his thoughts upon paper becomes at times an almost intolerable drudgery. . . .

Many persons who had written shorthand in the old way for years, became nearly discouraged at their slow progress. Those of them who have practised the system contained in this volume are, without exception, enthusiastic in its praise. Not only will the professional reporter, and they who take notes of addresses, be benefited by Mr. Lindsley's book, but also every literary man who has much occasion for making memoranda, or for writing what he has to deliver in public. The clergy, especially, will find the time and labor spent in mastering this system amply rewarded.   W. S. B.

THE RAPID WRITER QUARTERLY.

TABLE OF CONTENTS.

1871.

No. 6.—January. PAGE
Report on the New Short-hand, presented to the American Philological Society, New York .. 81
The Cherokee Alphabet 85
The Foundations of Despotism.— *Edward Everett* 86
Editorial Items 88
Correspondence 88
Literary Notices 91

No. 7.—April.
Professional Reporting 97
The Saxon Orthography 99
Rapid Writing 101
Chinese Printing 103
Foreign Correspondence.—Gabelsberger's Stenography 104

No. 8.—July.
The Origin of Words.—*Dan Saxon* 113

No. 8—*continued*. PAGE
What Clergymen are Learning .. 115
Undo the Heavy Burdens 116
Friendly Neutrality 117
Various Replies to a Practical Question 117
Editorial Items 120
Books and Periodicals 121

No. 9.—October.
The Origin of Words, No. 3, written in Illustration of a New Theory of the Meaning of the Ultimate Roots of Language 129
Our Mother Tongue 131
Editorial 136
Extracts from Correspondence .. 137
Literary Notices 138
Second Biennial Address, by the President of the American Tachygraphic Association 140

1872.

No. 10.—April. PAGE
Where was Fusang? An Inquiry into the Settlement of the Western Coast of America, and the Introduction of the Buddhist Religion by the Chinese in, or prior to, the Fifth Century of our Era. By Rev. Nathan Brown, D. D. 1
The Sun an Emblem. *Beecher* .. 13
Editorial Items 15
Answers to Correspondents 17
Literary Notices 18

No. 11.—October. PAGE
The English Phonography—How Managed 19
The Relm of Language. *Max Müller*. 22
Best Works for Study in Philology 23
Ministerial Work 24
Self and All. *Horace Greeley* .. 25
Elihu Burritt and the Vowel *U* .. 27
Moov Forward 28
EDITORIAL:—The Note-taker; To Old Phoneticians; Eight Styles of Phonography, &c........ 31

NOTICES OF THE PRESS.

"Contains much valuable information on short-hand writing." — *New Brunswick* (N. J.) *Daily Fredonian*.
"Full of choice articles on literary and philological subjects." — *American Baptist*, New York.
"Devoted to the introduction of a purely phonetic system of short hand writing. This subject cannot help receiving more attention." — *Springfield Republican*.
"Worthy of its reputation and its mission." — LANCASTER'S *Monthly Journal of Health*.

Single Numbers $0.12
The Numbers for 1871 and 1872 (Six Numbers) . .60
The Series Complete to 1873 (Eleven Numbers) . 1.00

Address, **THE RAPID WRITER**, ANDOVER, MASS.
For sale by OTIS CLAPP, 3 Beacon Street, Boston; and D. KIMBALL, Chicago, Ill., P. O. box 398.

TACHYGRAPHIC AND PHONETIC PUBLICATIONS.

THE ELEMENTS OF TACHYGRAPHY.

A Complete Treatise on the simplest style of the Art. The principles are illustrated by numerous examples of short-hand word-forms inserted in the text; by an extended series of exercises to be written by the student; and by reading lessons, beautifully engraved on copper. 120 pp. 12mo.

In cloth	Price, $1.75
Per dozen	16.80
In boards	1.50
Per dozen	14.40
Postage	12 cents a copy.

☞ The Third Edition now on sale, is printed on paper of the first quality, in the neatest manner.

THE TACHYGRAPHIC ALPHABET.

With directions for its use, and reading Lesson with Key	10
Per dozen	75

THE RAPID WRITER (Quarterly) for 1869, '70, and '71.

Single numbers	.10
Volume 1, bound in cloth (postage paid)	$1.25
Rapid Writer and Philological Magazine for January and April, 1873	.25

THE NOTE TAKER.

A full Treatise on the Second Style of Tachygraphy, to follow the "Elements," is now in course of publication, and will be issued soon, *complete.*

Bound in cloth	$2.75
Introductory specimen Number, now on sale	.40

ADDRESS,

OTIS CLAPP & SON,
No. 31 Beacon Street, Boston

D. KIMBALL, Box 398, Chicago, Ill.

www.ingramcontent.com/pod-product-compliance
Lightning Source LLC
Chambersburg PA
CBHW030900170426
43193CB00009BA/692